How to cope with too many stressors

Janet Haines
Mandy Matthewson

Acknowledgements:
Steven Haines
Robyn Cartledge
Coverart designed by Freepik
(www.freepik.com)

This workbook offers suggestions on how to cope with dealing with too many stressors. We do not guarantee that these suggested strategies will resolve all psychological symptoms. You may wish to seek alternative assistance from a mental health professional.

How to cope with too many stressors
Janet Haines & Mandy Matthewson
Copyright © 2025
ISBN: 978-1-923573-17-8

About the authors

Dr Janet Haines has a PhD in Clinical Psychology and has worked as an academic and researcher for 17 years, and in private practice for 30 years helping people facing life problems.

Dr Mandy Matthewson is a Clinical Psychologist, educator and researcher with more than two decades of experience supporting people through life's toughest challenges.

For S, who demonstrated determination and humour
in the face of overwhelming demand.

Table of contents

Table of contents 5
Introduction 7
A funny thing happened on your way to coping 8
What happened in the lead up to not coping well? 9
    What happens then? 11
Why did this happen? 12
What happens when I am tipped over the top? 14
The problem of attention and concentration 17
    How these problems manifest 17
    Causes of the problem 18
    How can I fix this? 20
What can I do about it? 21
    Exercises to quiet your mind and your anxiety 27
Manage your disturbed sleep 33
    What can I do about my sleep problems? 35
Expectations, demands and preferences 37
    Setting expectations 37
    Language you use when talking to yourself 38
    Reframe your expectations in terms of preferences not demands 40
Reprioritising and managing your time 43
    Prioritise what you need to do 43
    Break down your high priority, important tasks 46
    Avoid distractions and deals 47
    How to make time when you seem to have none 47
Changing your thinking 50
    How are our thoughts affected? 50
    Core beliefs 50
    Cognitive errors 51
    Why do we think in unhelpful ways? 62
    Underlying assumptions of logical errors 64
    Understanding automatic thoughts 67
    Catching automatic thoughts 68
    Understanding and noticing logical errors 70

- Reframing your thoughts (cognitive restructuring) 72
- Making the restructured thinking habitual 76
- Targeting the assumptions 77

Improving your coping skills 80
- Coping 80
- Problem-focused coping vs. emotion-focused coping 80
- Problem-approach vs. problem-avoidance copers 81
- Identifying your preferred coping style 84
- Building your coping repertoire 87

Understand your rights 96

Assertive negotiation 100
- Asking for change 100
- Negotiating for what you want 103

Achieving some balance 105
- Values clarification exercise for choosing preferred activities 105

Some final points 108

Additional reading 109

Introduction

We cope with significant life stressors all the time, and usually, we do this without too much trouble. However, problems can develop when too many stressful things happen at once, and we have to deal with them all. This workbook aims to help you cope when you feel overwhelmed by life, work and the demands being placed on you. It will explain how things went wrong and what you can do to make it better.

You may consider yourself to be one of those people who copes pretty well with problem situations and the stressors you face. This is probably true. Certainly, you would be the best judge of how you typically cope. However, everyone has a point beyond which their usual coping methods will fail them. This is true of everyone, even if that has never happened before. The fact that you are currently experiencing anxiety or stress should not shake your confidence about your general capacity to cope.

A funny thing happened on your way to coping

Even if you are a person who normally copes well with the demands placed on you, a point can be reached where those challenges exceed your capacity to cope. But the way we cope can be confusing at times. You would think that the point beyond which you cannot cope would be clearly defined. That is, you might think you can cope with two things, or three… or four things, but beyond that, it would be expected that you will not cope. Of course, it does not work that way.

You will find that sometimes you can cope with lots of things going on, but sometimes you cannot cope. This is because our ability to cope fluctuates across time and circumstance. That is, some days we are better copers, or at other times in our lives, we are poorer copers than we are at other times. Sometimes, we are quite successful at dealing with big problems, but then we find ourselves unable to cope when we are faced with an additional small problem. So, while it can be true that you generally cope well, we do accept that there are times when things do not work out quite as well.

Your belief in your capacity to cope with anything that comes your way can cause you problems. You can take on more and more, either because of the circumstance of the situation you are in or because of your character. Whatever the reason, when asked to do more, you do not say no. As a result of your belief that you can always cope, you just put your head down and keep trying to deal with excessive and increased demands on you. Unfortunately, there comes a point when the demands exceed your capacity to cope.

What happened in the lead up to not coping well?

It is reasonable to ask yourself what was going on that caused you to stop coping well. How did this period of not coping in your usual way get started? There are lots of ways things can develop leading up to the point where you stop coping as effectively as you would typically.

You might suddenly be faced with lots of things to do. These usually are things that are outside your normal routine. So, you can go from managing your life well to suddenly being overwhelmed. Let's consider an example.

> *Michael felt overwhelmed. He felt more overwhelmed than he remembered ever feeling before. Problems started when his wife, Laura, badly broke her leg when she slipped when she was running through the rain and ended up falling down some stairs. Michael had to take care of his wife. He also had to take over most of the household chores, including the cooking, and he had to get the children ready for school. He had to take the children to and from school and to their various activities outside of school hours. Although his boss was sympathetic, he said he couldn't really afford to have Michael away from work. So, Michael tried to do everything at home, attend to his wife's and children's needs, and keep doing his job. In an effort to do everything, he reduced the number of hours he spent at work but still tried to do the same amount of work as he was normally expected to do. After a few weeks of this, Michael found he was not sleeping well despite being exhausted. He felt anxious all the time, and he was concerned that he was going to fail to do something he should have remembered.*

Although things like this happen, it can also be the case that things can build up over time to a point where a person is no longer able to cope. In this case, there is no one point where you realise that you have taken on too much until you suddenly find you cannot cope. Consider this example.

> *Natalie found herself sitting on the side of her bed one morning, unable to force herself to get ready for work. She felt anxious and overwhelmed. No amount of telling herself she had to go to work seemed to motivate her to take that first step to get ready. It was like she was frozen on the spot. In the lead up to that morning, Natalie had taken on quite a lot at work. Her colleague had taken some time off work, and Natalie agreed to cover her duties while still maintaining her own workload. That colleague then suddenly resigned, so the length of time Natalie was expected to undertake the work of two positions was extended while a replacement for the colleague could be found. Natalie prided herself on hard work, but the demands placed on her were excessive. Increasingly, she found herself working longer hours. Other activities that Natalie usually engaged in outside of work were let go in favour of getting all the work done she was expected to undertake. The*

> *burden of covering this excessive workload continued until Natalie froze on the side of her bed and couldn't force herself to go to work.*

The impact of this demand can go unnoticed until it reaches a point where it can no longer be tolerated. This build-up of stress can be understood to be insidious because the person thinks they are managing until the point where they can no longer do so.

The failure to cope may be associated with a period of time when you are not in top form physically, or you are trying to recover from an illness, even a minor one. That is, you could cope with the additional demands until you are not feeling physically well. The physical illness can cause you to think less clearly, making it even more difficult to deal with all the challenges you are facing.

> *Angela is a busy, working, single mother of two primary school-aged children. Others often expressed their amazement that Angela could do all that she did. She would get up early while the children still slept to prepare for the day. She would take the children to school, then head straight off to work. She was employed in a job that meant she was on her feet all day. She would then pick up the children from after-school care. Her evenings were spent helping and caring for her children and keeping the house in order. She also cared for her ageing parents, helping them with household tasks and shopping. Angela was also fond of her elderly neighbour, and she would try to keep her neighbour's garden in order and make sure his garbage can was taken out on rubbish collection day. She would often cook for him. She would sew her children's clothes and knit their jumpers. There was no time left for Angela, but she felt her routine worked well and her children were happy. But Angela then picked up a virus she could not shake. Her symptoms were not debilitating, but she felt more tired than she ever remembered feeling. She found she could not keep up the pace of her daily life. Her doctor suggested she rest, but there was no one to take on the responsibilities she faced every day. She felt she had no choice but to battle on. However, that was easier said than done. Angela found herself becoming tearful over the smallest of things and anxious about the demands being placed on her. Although she hoped she would feel better soon, she didn't know what she was going to do in the meantime.*

The failure to cope in your usual way may be caused by a small number of bigger stressors or by a large number of smaller stressors. Whatever the build-up, the final trigger that could tip you over the edge may not necessarily be a big thing. Just one more small stressor is sufficient to cause you to reach your limit.

What happens then?

Whatever the pattern of the lead up to not being able to cope, you reach a point where you tip over the edge. At this point, you become anxious and unable to cope in your usual way. Your normal ways of coping do not seem to work.

Earlier in this process, you may just try harder to cope. You may put your head down and push forward, trying hard to stay on top of the demands being placed on you. However, you can reach a point where stress overwhelms you.

At this point, you stop functioning in the way you would normally. You might try to push yourself more and carry on, but this becomes increasingly difficult. You then reach your limit, and you simply cannot do this anymore. It is at this point that intense and uncomfortable anxiety symptoms develop. Your problem-solving strategies no longer work, and you cannot see a way out of the situation you find yourself in.

Why did this happen?

You may find that you reached a point of not being able to cope. This happened because you had to deal with too many things, or the things you were dealing with were too stressful, and this went on for too long. There are some things you need to know to understand why this is a problem.

To start, human beings have a range of nervous system arousal within which we function the best. This range is quite large, from low in the range when we are very relaxed to high in the range when our nervous system is most 'revved up'. Pictured below is a diagram of this arousal range. The range within which we function best is known as the *window of tolerance*.

Within this window of tolerance, you have the flexibility to respond to the demands being placed on you. In this way, your arousal level will increase when you are faced with a demand and then decrease when that demand is over. As long as your arousal stays within this window, you will respond well to pressures placed on you.

If your arousal level drops below the lowest point of that range, you will enter a state of hypoarousal. In this state, you will feel slowed down and lethargic. Your functioning at this point will be inadequate, and your ability to respond to demands will be poor. If your arousal increases beyond the ceiling level, you will enter a state of hyperarousal. When this occurs, you can feel too aroused and can feel anxious and panicky. Your functioning will be impacted, and your ability to cope with pressures will deteriorate.

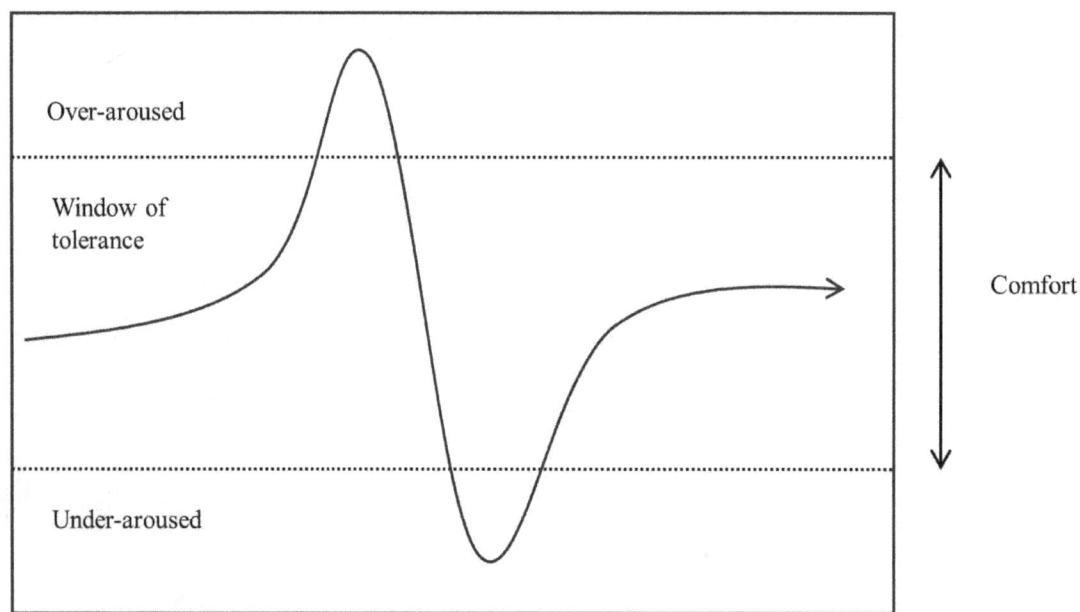

Figure 1: A diagram of the window of tolerance.

When you have been too stressed for too long but are still managing to cope, your arousal level creeps up from an optimal level of arousal in the middle of the window of tolerance to the upper extreme. You will find that you cannot or do not reduce that high level of arousal, even when you should be able to let go. This is why people cannot sleep well when they are under pressure. They can never relax enough for their arousal to decrease to a comfortable state. It just stays up near the upper limit of this window of tolerance. Your 'baseline' arousal level, which is the starting point from which you respond to life demands, is high up in the range instead of midway or lower in the window of tolerance.

In this way, your arousal level remains elevated. You barely notice this because it starts to feel normal to be under that much stress with your arousal level that high. But a problem exists. When any other thing occurs to which you have to respond, your arousal level will increase to deal with that additional demand being placed on you. It is normal for your arousal to increase to meet everyday challenges. However, with the starting point of your arousal level, or your baseline arousal level, being already so high, you have no room to move. Any increase in arousal will push you through the ceiling and into an uncomfortable and unpleasant hyperaroused state. You will experience anxiety as a result.

Your high starting point gives you no flexibility to respond or react to even minor additional stressors. So, the ways you normally cope with demanding situations fail because you have moved out of the range where you can successfully apply your usual coping strategies and where your nervous system can flexibly respond to normal day-to-day stressors.

What happens when I am tipped over the top?

When your arousal level pushes beyond the ceiling in your window of tolerance or comfortable arousal level range, your nervous system responds as if you are under immediate threat. We will explain here what you experience when this occurs.

Your autonomic nervous system (ANS) is the part of your nervous system that drives your functioning. It regulates your heart rate and temperature and makes other adjustments that are required for you to function on a moment-by-moment basis.

Your ANS is divided into two parts: the parasympathetic nervous system and the sympathetic nervous system. Your parasympathetic nervous system is the part of your ANS that should be driving you most of the time. It makes sure everything is ticking along so that your body gets what it needs and you can function well.

Your sympathetic nervous system has a specialised function. It is your self-protection system that automatically activates when you are under threat. So, if you were crossing the road and a truck came screaming around the corner, your sympathetic nervous system would activate so that you could quickly and efficiently move out of the way of the truck and reach safety. Adrenaline would release into your system, causing your hands to shake and your heart rate to increase, but you would reach the safety of the footpath on the other side of the road, and you would be fine. Your brain would then recognise that you were safe, and your sympathetic nervous system would turn off, and your parasympathetic nervous system would take over again.

Your sympathetic nervous system is attuned to your brain perceiving signs of threat. It activates when you are at risk of harm and prepares you to deal with that threat. It is an effective self-protection system when you are under threat. Unfortunately, for people who develop an overly sensitive sympathetic nervous system or for people with too many things going on in their lives, their sympathetic nervous system will activate at the slightest indication that something is wrong and will prepare them to deal with the threat. This can occur even when there really is no threat to manage. This is what happens when you are anxious in the absence of an obvious cause of your anxiety. In effect, your brain cannot distinguish between an external threat (e.g., a truck coming around the corner) and an internal threat (e.g., you thinking worrying or anxiety-provoking thoughts) or when you have pushed yourself too far and given yourself too much to do. An overly sensitive nervous system will rely on its self-defence mechanism to protect you from perceived harm.

Your nervous system will also react to crises in your life that do not present the same level of threat. Although having too much to do is stressful, this, in itself, is not physically threatening to you. Nevertheless, your sympathetic nervous system can be triggered by the demands on you. As stated, your brain cannot always distinguish between an external threat to your physical integrity and the internally generated reaction to the threat to your emotional well-being or being overloaded with too many things to do.

Below is a table providing an overview of the activities of the parasympathetic and sympathetic nervous systems.

Table 1: The functions of the parasympathetic and sympathetic nervous systems.

	Parasympathetic	Sympathetic
Eyes	Constricts pupils	Dilates pupils
Salivary glands	Stimulates salivation	Inhibits salivation
Heart	Slows heartbeat	Accelerates heartbeat
Lungs	Constricts bronchi	Dilates bronchi
Stomach	Stimulates digestion	Inhibits digestion
Liver	Stimulates bile release	Simulates glucose release
Kidneys		Stimulates release of adrenaline and noradrenaline*
Intestines	Stimulates peristalsis and secretion	Inhibits peristalsis and secretion
Bladder	Contracts bladder	Relaxes bladder

* Also known as epinephrine and norepinephrine.

When your sympathetic nervous system is activated, a series of physical changes occur that make sense if they are in response to a threat to your physical integrity. Some of these changes are listed below.

> Adrenaline is released so that you are alert and in a heightened state, ready to deal with the threat. This causes your heart rate to increase and can cause your hands, or even your whole body, to shake.
>
> Your hearing and your eyesight become better than normal. Everything sounds louder than it really is, and it is difficult to tolerate lots of light and movement. This is why anxious people tend to avoid places like supermarkets. Too much noise, too much light, and too much movement can be overwhelming when you feel anxious. Anxious people tend to tolerate these things poorly because of the acuteness of their senses when their sympathetic nervous systems are activated. It helps to have really

good hearing and eyesight if you are being threatened, but it does not help if you are just trying to engage in daily activities.

In our view, the most amazing thing that happens is that your sympathetic nervous system shuts down the systems it does not need to be using. For example, when under threat, your body needs to produce lots of glucose for energy, so it stimulates glucose production. In a heightened state of arousal, your body burns through the glucose that is produced. To allow for greater availability of glucose, other systems that are not needed are shut down. In particular, your sympathetic nervous system shuts down your gastrointestinal system (e.g., inhibits digestion and inhibits peristalsis and secretion, with peristalsis referring to the contraction of the muscles that push forward the contents of your digestive tract). This is all right if it is shut down for the period of time it takes for you to deal with a truck coming around the corner. Your body copes less well with your gastrointestinal system not functioning if the sympathetic nervous system activation is prolonged. You can lose your appetite, experience nausea, develop diarrhoea or constipation, and you can experience difficulty eating, or you will overeat to try to control the uncomfortable state of your digestive system.

All of these symptoms make sense if you are under threat but become a problem if the activation of your sympathetic nervous system is prolonged. Also, when your sympathetic nervous system is activated for reasons other than obvious threat, you can develop a sense of imminent danger just because your sympathetic nervous system has taken over your functioning. When your sympathetic nervous system is activated, your brain will interpret this as a sign that something is wrong. This explains why you feel this overwhelming sense that something terrible is going to happen.

Later, we will introduce some straightforward ways you can bring your sympathetic nervous system under better control so your anxiety and fear are reduced. You can learn to control the messages being received because you are worried so that the message is not misinterpreted, and you can avoid the sense that something terrible is going to happen. However, before we do that, there is one other consequence of prolonged, increased arousal that needs to be considered.

The problem of attention and concentration

One problem that is reported regularly by people who are in an anxious state is that their attention and concentration has been affected. This is also true for people who have been overwhelmed by the stressors in their life.

We know that problems of attention and concentration occur with particular conditions, such as Attention Deficit Hyperactivity Disorder and Generalised Anxiety Disorder. However, excessive stress can produce the same problems for people. Remember, excessive demands on you push your nervous system arousal up towards the top of your window of tolerance. It is at this point that you start to notice these types of difficulties.

How these problems manifest

There are lots of ways in which these problems manifest. At first, you would probably notice difficulty remembering things. Lots of people attribute the problems of attention and concentration to memory deficits and they start to worry there is something wrong with their memory. Below are some examples of the ways in which problems of attention and concentration appear.

What was I saying?

You might forget what you about to say. You will be halfway through a sentence when you forget what you were planning to say next. You can start to give an account of an experience and then fail to recall the end of the story, even though it is something known to you. Although everyone experiences these problems from time to time, it is the frequency with which they occur when you are stressed that can disturb you.

Losing track

You might lose track of what you are reading or programmes you are watching on television. This is a common complaint. Overly stressed people will start reading and, even though they continue to read, they realise they cannot recall what they just read and will have to start again. This is particularly problematic for people who have to read things as part of their job or who read as a form of relaxation. The same thing can happen when watching a programme. The point or plot of what you are watching is lost.

What was I doing?

You might lose track of what you are doing or where you were going and what you intended to do when you got there. This can be frustrating. You might walk into a room with seemingly clear intention to do something, but them become completely confused about why you went into the room in the first instance. People with problems of attention and concentration will report going into a shop to buy a couple of items but leave without those items because they could not recall what they intended to buy so they bought something else instead. This manifestation of the problem can cause you to waste time having to backtrack to try to remember what it was you were doing or revisit places you have already been where you failed to do what you set out to do.

Making mistakes

These problems of attention and concentration can cause you to make mistakes that you would not normally make. You lose track of what you are doing and fail to notice that you have missed something or entered the wrong information or made some other simple error. Sometimes, these simple errors can set off a series of ongoing errors that end up creating a bigger problem than making a simple error would suggest would occur. To overcome the problem, people will either slow down or check and re-check what they have done. These are time consuming activities that further burden you when your time is already taken up with all the things you have to do.

Causes of the problem

The simple answer to why you are having problems with attention and concentration is that you are too stressed and your arousal level is too high. However, this does not really tell you what it is about being too stressed or too aroused that results in attention and concentration difficulties. We need to break it down to consider the individual factors that impact on the development of these problems.

Cognitive load

Firstly, the problems of attention and centration and, therefore, memory, occur because of the cognitive load being experienced by your brain. Fundamentally, you have too many things to think about at once and your brain tries to give them all some attention. This reduces how much attention can be directed to any one thing. Even when you try to concentrate on one thing, your brain still recognises that there are lots of other things on your mind and checks to make sure that there is nothing that needs to be attended to with these other things.

Intrusive thoughts

The issue with cognitive load then causes you to experience intrusive thoughts about things that are not currently of central concern to you. With your brain trying to keep track of everything that is going on, you will be distracted by 'reminder' thoughts that are a reflection of the fact that your brain has focused briefly on one of the other multitude of things you have to do. These types of thoughts enter your mind in one of two ways. They either briefly appear but are enough to interfere with your concentration on what you are currently doing. Alternatively, the intrusion of the 'reminder' thought can distract you and your concentration on the thing you are currently doing is lost.

Attentional bias

Your brain has what is known as attentional bias. That is, it pays attention to the things that are most important to your survival. With a survival bias, your brain may draw your attention to things that seem particularly stressful or cause you to focus on how you are feeling rather than on what you need to be doing. With a survival bias, most of your attention will not be devoted to things such as the demands of your job. A survival bias allows your brain to recognise that there are indicators that you are stressed and to focus on the things you most need to be aware of in a crisis. These things are not the shopping list or the spreadsheet you might be working on in your job or the book you are reading.

Executive functioning

Executive functioning is the term used to describe the processes that take place in your brain that help you plan, organise and set goals and work towards them. The various components of your executive functioning include (a) planning and organisation (prioritising tasks, setting goals, and organising materials); (b) working memory (holding information and manipulating it in your mind); (c) inhibition (controlling impulses and controlling thoughts and actions); (d) attention (focusing of specific things and shifting attention from one thing to another); and (e) cognitive flexibility (easily adapting to changing circumstances and the ability to adjust plans).

Stress and anxiety have the following influences on your executive functioning. They reduce *attentional control* making it hard to filter out things that can distract you. This causes you to have trouble concentrating. They cause you to *overestimate threat.* In this way, you perceive situations as more threatening or dangerous than is actually the case. They cause you to experience difficulty in *goal-oriented behaviour.* When stressed, you will find it harder to set goals and pursue them in an effective manner. The effect of stress on your executive functioning *impairs decision-making.* It is harder to decide what to do so the quality of your decision-making is poorer than it would be otherwise. It has an influence on *self-regulation.* It is hard to keep a good control of your emotional state, your thoughts and your actions.

All of these influences make it harder to you to attend to what you are doing and concentrate on the things that need your attention. It can make you feel less capable and more uncertain.

How can I fix this?

The good news is that the same strategies that are used to manage your nervous system arousal will resolve the problems of attention and concentration. Let's consider these types of strategies next.

What can I do about it?

Your goal should be to get your nervous system back under control. Dealing with the challenges you are facing likely pushed your arousal level to the upper limits of your window of tolerance. Extra demands, even minor ones, then cause your arousal level to move beyond the ceiling of the window of tolerance and uncomfortable and unpleasant anxiety symptoms are then experienced and your attention and concentration are affected.

You need to aim to bring your optimal arousal level down to at least the middle of the window of tolerance, with a baseline or starting point, when you are at your most relaxed, to the lower end of that range. You need to teach your nervous system to have a better starting point and a better optimal arousal level.

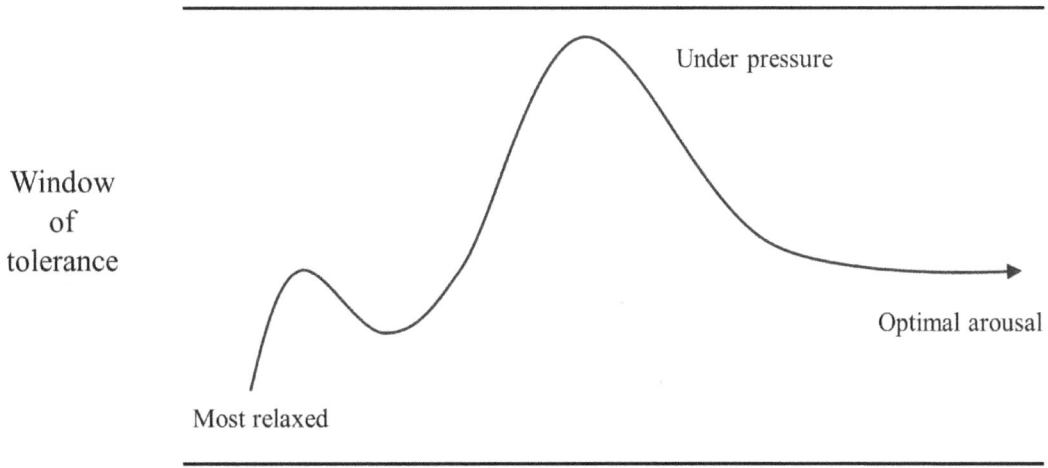

Figure 2: A diagram of an optimal level of arousal.

How do you achieve this? Consider the following. When you are in an elevated or heightened state, at the top of your window of tolerance or beyond it, your heart rate increases and your breathing changes. Your heart rate elevation can be caused by a release of adrenaline that occurs when your sympathetic nervous system is triggered. This can be very uncomfortable, and it feels like there is very little you can do about it.

However, your breathing changes contribute to the elevation in your heart rate. When people are stressed, their breathing tends to be rapid and shallow. You can liken this pattern of breathing to the waves on top of the water. Form a picture in your mind of the way a child draws waves. When we are stressed, we tend to breathe in sharply, then breathe out quickly and then breathe in again quickly. You tend not to breathe all the way out before you breathe in again. This inhalation-exhalation pattern is what affects your heart rate.

In contrast, when we are relaxed, your breathing tends to be deeper and slower and has a pattern than is similar to the swell in the ocean. The inhalation-exhalation pattern is a comfortable breath-in followed by a long, slower breath-out. You do not breathe in again until you have breathed all the way out.

From the diagram below, you can see the pattern of anxious, rapid and shallow breathing on the top. Below that is the pattern of slower, deeper breathing that is characteristic of a more relaxed state.

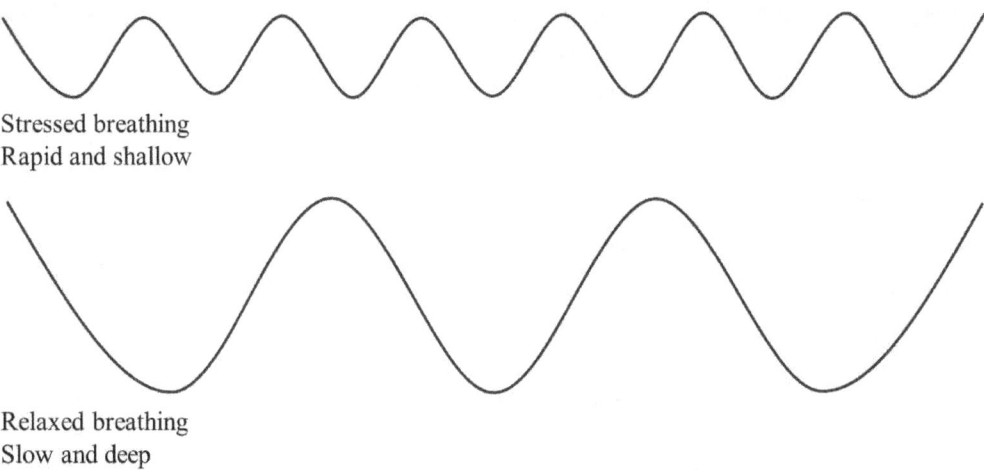

Figure 3: A comparison between stressed and relaxed breathing.

The reason your breathing pattern affects your heart rate is because these two things are linked. Under normal, stress-free conditions, your heart rate increases as you breathe in and then slows as you breathe out. This is normal. When you are stressed and your respiration rate increases and your breathing is shallower, you heart rate does not have a chance to slow before you breathe in again. Therefore, your heart rate is elevated and stays up.

Let's, for a moment, go back to the truck speeding around the corner, threatening to run you over. Your sympathetic nervous system is activated, allowing you to be in the right physical state to move quickly out of harm's way and protect yourself. When you get to the other side of the road, the truck goes past and you are unharmed, your brain registers these experiences and your sympathetic nervous system turns off, and your parasympathetic nervous system takes over. This is because reaching the other side of the road and seeing the truck pass you by are safety signals. Your brain interprets these signs as indicators that you are going to be all right.

Of course, no such safety signals are available when you are doing too much, sitting in your loungeroom worrying, or shopping at the supermarket. They are not that sort of event. Your brain would struggle to identify safety indicators because they do not exist in that sort of form. What you can do is offer your brain a safety signal but of a different type.

You can send a message that everything is all right by deliberately slowing your heart rate from its elevated rate to a more normal rate for you. Although it sounds difficult to achieve, controlling your heart rate is actually a reasonably straightforward undertaking. If you slow your breathing and lengthen your exhalation until you have breathed all the way out before breathing back in, your heart rate will come into line, and your heart rate will go down.

To use our waves and ocean swell analogy, the aim is to change the pattern of your breathing from waves on the top of the water to a pattern like the swell in the ocean, where the water is lifted up and then put back down as the swell passes. You are aiming for an easy, comfortable breath in, followed by a long, slow breath out.

The ideal situation is to breathe out for twice as long as it takes you to breathe in. Lengthening your breath out requires that you slow the amount of air you breathe out so that you can breathe out for longer. You should aim to breathe all the way out, emptying your lungs, before you gently and comfortably breathe back in.

This pattern of breathing should result in a slowed heart rate and a subsequent reduction in that sense of anxiety or crisis that occurs when your sympathetic nervous system is triggered. This occurs because your brain interprets the reduction in heart rate and the change in breathing pattern as a signal that the crisis is over.

Let's consider a simple exercise to control your breathing by deepening your breaths and slowing them down.

	Slowing and controlling your breathing
1.	Without trying to change your breathing, just notice for a moment the pattern of your inhalations and exhalations.
2.	Now, take a comfortable breath in. It does not have to be too deep, rather just a comfortable breath.
3.	Now, breathe out, slowing the amount of air you exhale and lengthening your breath as a result.
4.	When your lungs feel empty of air, gently and comfortably breathe back in.
5.	As you breathe, practice lengthening your exhalation just a bit. You may also deepen your breath in slightly. Keep in mind the picture of the ocean swell if this helps.
6.	Practice this pattern of breathing for as long as you feel comfortable.

Exercise available at elemen.com.au

There is another element that you can add to this breathing exercise that may help with your ultimate goal of reducing your anxiety and signalling your sympathetic nervous system to turn off so your parasympathetic nervous system can do its job. You can include in this breathing exercise the element of reducing your muscle tension.

People who are stressed tend to have tense muscles. Although this muscle tension can occur anywhere in the body, common sites include the forehead and scalp, neck, jaw, shoulders, and chest. The increased muscle tension contributes to the overall sense of readiness to deal with threat. On the downside, tense muscles can cause headaches, chest and other pain.

If tense muscles present a significant problem for you, then a progressive muscle relaxation exercise may help. A general overview of this technique is provided below. More comprehensive versions are available online. However, another easy strategy is to link the relaxation of muscles with the breathing exercise.

As you breathe out, just relax your muscles in places where they feel tight and tense. You do not have to achieve marked muscle relaxation to experience a noticeable difference. Just drop your shoulders, relax your jaw, smooth your forehead or relax your stomach muscles. Aim for a gentle relaxation of tight muscles as you exhale.

The combination of breathing exercise and muscle relaxation can be used even when the focus is on controlling your breathing. You can also use the combined technique when your primary focus is on troubling muscle tension. In combination, the techniques can help with either target.

	Combined breathing and muscle relaxation technique
1.	Take a comfortable breath in. It does not have to be too deep, rather just a comfortable breath.
2.	Now, breathe out, slowing the amount of air you exhale and lengthening your breath as a result. As you breathe out, drop your shoulders, relax your jaw, smooth your forehead and relax your abdominal muscles.
3.	When your lungs feel empty of air, gently and comfortably breathe back in.
4.	As you breathe, practice lengthening your exhalation just a bit. You may also deepen your breath in slightly. Keep in mind the picture of the ocean swell if this helps. Continue to relax your muscles slightly on each exhalation.
5.	Practice this pattern of breathing and muscle relaxation for as long as you feel comfortable.

Exercise available at elemen.com.au

As stated, if muscle tension presents you with a significant problem, you may wish to try a method of progressive muscle relaxation. This technique involves tensing your muscles then relaxing them. Tensing your muscles before relaxing them has a number of purposes. It helps you to clearly identify where the tension in your body is located. It helps you feel the difference between a tense muscle and a relaxed one, which is helpful when the muscle has been tense for a long time. Finally, tensing the muscle first helps to induce deeper relaxation in that muscle when you relax it.

We will start with a longer version that will help you learn the technique. You can then change to a shorter version that we describe below.

	Progressive muscle relaxation (longer version)
1.	Choose a comfortable place where it is quiet. Lay down or sit in a comfortable position with your feet flat on the floor.
2.	Now, clench both your fists… tighter and tighter. Notice the tension in your muscles. Keep them clenched for about 10 seconds. Now relax. Feel your muscles relax. Notice the difference between the tension and relaxation. Repeat the procedure with your fists and notice the difference between tension and relaxation.
3.	Now, bend your elbows of both arms and tense your biceps. Hold the tension. Now relax. Notice the difference between tension and relaxation. Repeat the procedure with your elbows bent and biceps tensed. Pay attention to the changes from tension to relaxation.
4.	Now, frown as hard as you can. Notice the tension in your forehead. Hold the tension. Now relax. Notice the difference you feel after you have released the tension.
5.	Now, frown again as hard as you can. Hold the tension, then release it. Notice the contrast between tension and relaxation.
6.	Now, close your eyes and squint them tightly. Hold the tension then relax. Allow your eyes to feel a comfortable, relaxed state. Notice the change. Repeat by closing your eyes and squinting then relaxing, letting go of the tension.
7.	Now, clench your jaw. Bite down hard. Notice the tension throughout your jaw. Now, relax your jaw, allowing your teeth to fall apart slightly. Notice the feeling of relaxation. Repeat this exercise with your jaw.
8.	Now, press your tongue hard against the roof of your mouth. Hold it there. Feel the tension at the back of your mouth. Now relax. Notice the difference between the tension and relaxation. Repeat the exercise with your tongue.
9.	Now, purse your lips, pushing them out into an 'O' shape. Hold them there. Now, release the tension and relax. Notice how your mouth feels now that it is relaxed. Repeat the exercise with your lips.

10.	Now, press your head back as far as it will comfortably go. Hold onto the tension. Roll your head from the right to the left, allowing the focus of the tension to change. Now relax. Feel the difference between the tension in your neck and the relaxation. Repeat the exercise by pressing your head back.
11.	Now, bring your head forward with your chin on your chest. Feel the tension in your throat and the back of your neck. Hold the tension, then relax and allow your head to return to a comfortable position. Repeat the exercise by bringing your head forward.
12.	Now, shrug your shoulders, bringing your shoulders up and allowing your head to hunch down between them. Hold the tension. Now relax and notice the difference between tension and relaxation.
13.	Now, breathe in deeply and hold your breath. Hold it. Now allow yourself to gently exhale, letting go of tension as you breathe out. Feel your body relax. Repeat the exercise, breathing in then gently letting go.
14.	Now, tense your stomach muscles. Hold onto the tension. Now relax. Let your stomach muscles relax and appreciate that feeling. Repeat the exercise with your stomach muscles.
15.	Now, arch your back without straining. Hold onto the tension. Now let it go. Notice the change in your muscles. Now repeat the exercise by arching your back.
16.	Now, tighten your buttocks and thighs. Press down on your heels to flex your thigh muscles. Hold onto the tension. Now relax and notice the difference. Repeat the exercise
17.	Now, curl your toes downward to cause your calves to tense. Hold onto the tension. Now relax. Repeat the exercise.
18.	Now, draw your toes upward, causing your shins to feel tense. Pay attention to the tension. Now relax. Repeat the exercise.
19.	Now, scan your body. Notice if there are any tense spots. Repeat the exercise in that area.
20.	Enjoy the more relaxed feeling throughout your entire body. When you are ready, slowly return to your normal activities, holding on to that feeling of relaxation.

Exercise available at elemen.com.au

Once you have learned the technique, you can use a shorter version. You may prefer to just focus on the areas of your body that are particularly tense. It is certainly the case that some people tend to carry their muscle tension in one or two areas. Here is a shorter version that will allow you to tailor the procedure to suit your own needs.

	Relaxing using progressive muscle relaxation (short version)
1.	Choose a comfortable place where it is quiet. Lay down or sit in a comfortable position with your feet flat on the floor.
2.	Begin to work your way through groups of muscles by tensing them and relaxing them. For example, if you start with your forehead, tighten the muscles in your forehead by frowning. Hold for a few moments (10-15 seconds), then release, allowing the muscle in your forehead to relax, enjoying that experience for about 60 seconds. Notice the difference between the tension and the relaxation.
3.	Then, move on to the next group of muscles. You can work through groups of muscles from the top of your head to the tips of your toes, or you can select areas of your body that present a particular problem of tension for you.
4.	Repeat the process until you have worked your way through the groups of muscles you have selected.
5.	Repeat that process again, first tensing the muscles, holding that tension for five to ten seconds, and then relaxing those muscles.

Exercise available at elemen.com.au

So, controlling your breathing and, thus, lowering your heart rate will help you feel less anxious, as will reducing your muscle tension. However, there are other approaches you can take to anxiety management.

Exercises to quiet your mind and your anxiety

One of the problems with being anxious and 'revved up' is that your mind fills up with anxiety-provoking thoughts. When there are too many things going on in your life, you cannot seem to stop thinking in an endless stream of anxiety-provoking thoughts. This makes it very difficult to get your nervous system back under control. The thoughts racing through your mind do not allow you to relax. So, included here are some exercises that should help you settle your mind.

The first exercises aim to teach you to self-soothe. If you can learn to settle yourself, the racing thoughts in your mind may follow. The quieter your nervous system, the less active your mind is with anxiety-provoking thoughts.

What you are aiming to do is find ways to soothe yourself. Most of us can understand how we go about soothing an upset child. We might hold and rock a distressed child and say soothing things. What you are looking for are adult versions of self-soothing strategies that will help to alleviate your distressed state.

The goal of developing self-soothing strategies is to create for yourself some moments of less distress. The strategies are aimed at reducing your heightened state to a more manageable level. They allow your nervous system arousal level to be brought back under your control. So, strategies that allow you to focus on the here and now are the ones that will allow you to choose to be in a quieter state with a greater sense of peace of mind.

Consider the proposed self-soothing strategies listed below and select ones that you think might assist you. These may be things you have tried before or ones you feel might work for you. Some of these strategies require you to make an effort to seek out the means of engaging with them. However, others are using things that are readily available or easily obtained.

	Self-soothing strategies
	Take a shower or a warm bath. Focus your attention on the sensations created by the water. Enjoy the feeling of the water on your skin and the warmth of the water.
	Play with your pet or just stroke your dog's or cat's coat. Interacting with your pet has been demonstrated to be soothing for many pet owners.
	Change into your most comfortable clothes. Enjoy the feel of the fabric and the degree of comfort you feel from wearing these items of clothing.
	Go for a swim. Enjoy the sensation of being in the water. Allow those sensations to quiet your mind. Even if you are not a good swimmer, bobbing around in the water can produce the same sensations.
	Treat yourself to a massage if that appeals to you. Allow your muscles to relax and your mind to quiet.
	Listen to soothing music. Allow your attention to be directed to the music rather than have the music in the background.
	Listen to an audiobook, even if your distress makes it difficult to concentrate. Try to pay attention to each word that is spoken. If you lose track of the story, you can always return to the previous track and pick up the story again.

	Turn on the television or talkback radio and engage in listening to what is being broadcast. The goal here is to focus your attention on the conversations as they play out rather than selecting a programme you are excited to watch or listen to. It is the process of listening to others talking that is soothing.
	Listen to the sounds of water running. Again, the aim is to listen to the sounds of the water, stopping your mind from going to other intrusive thoughts. You can find the sound of running water in various places. You can visit a naturally occurring water course or waterfall. You could listen to running water from an outdoor garden fountain. However, you can also get an indoor personal fountain that can be used at any time. Alternatively, you can listen to recorded sounds of water running.
	Find something soothing to look at. This might be by the water or an outdoor space such as a park. It could be photographs or paintings that you find soothing or relaxing. The goal is to find something to look at that is engaging for you, and that you find relaxing and soothing.

Exercise available at elemen.com.au

Building on this notion of self-soothing, it is a good idea to be more present in your focus. If you give it some consideration, you will find that the thoughts racing through your mind when you are anxious typically are not related to what is happening here and now. Our thoughts tend to engage in time-travelling, that is, they are focused either on what has already happened or what is to come. They rarely focus on what is happening in the present moment when you are trying to relax.

Usually, at these times, nothing is happening that is worth worrying about. If you could deliberately spend more time focused on the here and now and less time on the past or future, you would have a better chance of relaxing and quieting your overly stimulated nervous system.

The notion of focusing on the here and now is based on mindfulness techniques. Mindfulness refers to your ability to be aware of your emotions, your physical state, your actions and your thoughts in a state of mind that is absent from judgment or criticism of your experience. Research has demonstrated that mindfulness helps you to control symptoms of anxiety, to control the distress caused by particular situations, to increase your capacity to relax, and to learn how to cope better with challenging situations.

Based on the notion of mindfulness, we have included some exercises you can use to quiet your mind by focusing on the here and now. To do this well, you may need to practice the skill. When you first learn these techniques, it is easy to become distracted and return to your racing thoughts. Do not worry if this happens. Just return to your exercise and continue.

Mindful listening	
1.	Sit in a comfortable place, preferably by yourself. If you wish, close your eyes.
2.	Start to focus your attention on the sounds around you.
3.	Notice the changes in the sounds from moment to moment.
4.	Notice the times between sounds when it is quiet.
5.	Focus your attention both on what is happening inside and outside.
6.	Pay attention to the sounds and nothing else. Do not make judgments about the sounds. Just acknowledge the sound then listen to the next one.
7.	If thoughts about other things come into your mind, put them to one side then return to listening to the sounds around you.
8.	Do this for a few minutes or until you are ready to stop.

Exercise available at elemen.com.au

Let's try another mindfulness exercise.

Mindful use of your senses	
Sight	Look around you. Allow your attention to be drawn to five things in your immediate environment that you might not normally pay any attention to. For example, this might be the way the fruit is sitting in the fruit bowl, the way your curtain is hanging, or the way your books are placed on your bookcase. Allow your attention to rest on each of these things. Keep your focus directed at the item, setting aside any other thoughts that come into your mind.
Touch	Bring your attention to four things you can feel at this moment in time. For example, it may be the feel of the sun on your skin, or the feel of the fabric of your clothes against your skin, or the feel of the chair underneath you, or the feel of the table surface where your hand is resting. Allow your attention to rest on each of these feelings. Keep your focus directed at each sense of touch, setting aside any other thoughts that come into your mind.

Hearing	Listen to the sounds in your surroundings. Notice three things you can hear. For example, you might hear the sounds of cars travelling along the road, the noise of the refrigerator, or the sound of the wind in the trees. Focus your attention on each of these sounds. If other thoughts come into your mind, let those thoughts go and return to focusing on the sounds you can hear.
Smell	Pay attention and search for two things you can smell. For example, you might be able to smell whatever you are cooking, the scent of plants in your garden, or the sea air if you live near the water. Keep your attention focused on each of these smells. If other distracting thoughts come into your mind, let these thoughts go and return to focusing on the things you can smell.
Taste	When you are eating, focus your attention on the tastes you are experiencing. For example, take a sip of your coffee and notice the taste. Bite into your sandwich and notice the flavours. Really pay attention to the flavours of the things you are tasting. If you become distracted, let go of these interfering thoughts and return to focusing on the things you are tasting.

Exercise available at elemen.com.au

And there is one last mindfulness exercise.

	Mindful walking
1.	As you are ready for your walk, stand still for a moment. Sense the weight on your feet as you stand there. Feel how your muscles are supporting you and maintaining your stability and balance. Notice your arms in a comfortable position of your choice (e.g., by your side or hands clasped, either at the front or at your back). Allow yourself to stand there, relaxed but alert.
2.	Begin to walk. Choose a comfortable pace, not too fast and not too slow. Pay attention to how your feet and legs feel (e.g., their heaviness or lightness, the energy, or even any pain). The way your legs and feet feel will form the focus of your attention. If you become distracted, return to focusing on your legs and feet.
3.	Pay attention to the way in which you lift your feet and place them back down on the surface on which you are walking. Notice how you lift your foot, swing your leg and place your foot down again ahead of where you were a moment before. Walk in a natural and relaxed manner. Move your arms in a way that feels normal for you.

4.	It is likely that your mind will wander as you walk along. Your attention will be drawn to what is around you or thoughts that come into your mind. Acknowledge that you have been distracted and return to focusing on the process of walking… the lifting of your foot, the swing of your leg and the placement of your foot in front of you. Just gently return your attention to the sensations of walking.
5.	You might focus on a point ahead of you. Focus on the steps you take as you move towards that point. One step at a time. Experience fully the sensations of walking.
6.	Keep walking mindfully until you reach your destination or the point where you decide to turn around and mindfully walk back to where you started.

Exercise available at elemen.com.au

You have been introduced here to ways to control your anxiety, reduce your arousal level, and quiet your mind. We need to consider one way, in particular, that being too stressed has an impact on you in terms of your arousal level and the anxious chatter in your mind. We are referring here to the effect on your sleep.

Manage your disturbed sleep

One of the consequences of your nervous system being revved up and having too many stressful thoughts is that your sleep can become disturbed. You can become fatigued as a consequence and it becomes more difficult for you to cope with the demands of your day.

There are three types of insomnia. You might experience any one or all three of these types of sleep problems.

Trouble going to sleep. This is where you are unable to go to sleep despite being tired. You toss and turn. Nothing seems to allow you to drift off to sleep.

Trouble staying asleep. This is where you repeatedly wake throughout the night but, after a period of time, you are able to go back to sleep.

Waking early and being unable to go back to sleep. This is where you wake early in the morning, and despite needing more sleep, you cannot return to sleep.

Each of these types of sleep problems is understandable if you take into consideration your stages of sleep.

Table 2: A description of the stages of sleep.

Stages of sleep	
Stage 1	This is a transitional stage from wakefulness to sleep. It is associated with very light sleep. During this stage, muscle activity slows down.
Stage 2	During this stage, your sleep starts to deepen. Your breathing pattern changes and slows as does your heart rate. Your body temperature drops slightly.
Stage 3	It is at this stage that deep sleep begins to be experienced. To signal the onset of deep sleep, your brain starts to generate slow delta waves.
Stage 4	This is when you are most deeply asleep. During this stage, your muscle activity is limited.
REM sleep	This refers to Rapid Eye Movement Sleep. It occurs when you are at the closest point to wakefulness. It is associated with vivid dreaming. During this stage, your heart rate increases.

Over the course of the night, you will cycle through these stages. For the first half or so of the night, you will cycle down into the deep sleep associated with stages 3 and 4. However, as the night progresses, the cycling pattern is lighter and does not involve deep sleep. This pattern is demonstrated in the diagram below. Periods of REM sleep occur at the point in the cycle when you are closest to waking.

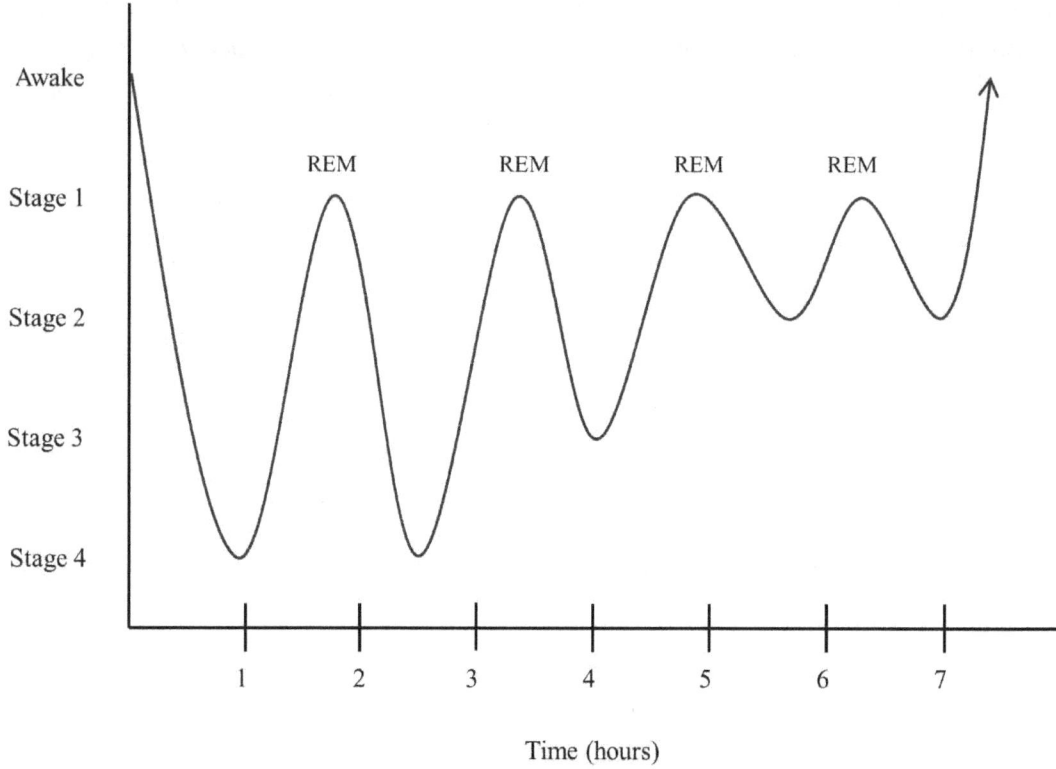

Figure 4: The cycles of sleep over the course of a sleep period.

When you have trouble falling asleep at the beginning of the night, you are struggling to enter into Stage 1 of sleep. This transitional stage is designed to pull you down into deeper sleep. Stage 1 allows you to do what your brain is inviting you to do, that is, drift off to sleep. Unfortunately, if you are stressed, your nervous system is generally too aroused to allow this to occur. Your nervous system fights against the urge to sleep. Your stressful thoughts are indicating to your brain that it is a good idea to stay awake in case something happens to which you need to respond.

When you have trouble staying asleep, you tend to wake up when your sleep cycle reaches those points where it is closest to wakefulness. In general, your nervous system is too aroused to allow you to stay asleep. Then, as soon as you wake, your mind turns to stressful thoughts that then keep you awake until you can get back to sleep. This can happen many times throughout the night.

When you are troubled by waking early and being unable to return to sleep, this usually occurs in the second part of the night when you have moved past the deep sleep cycles. Your sleep is lighter, and when your nervous system is too aroused, and you come close to wakefulness, you become completely awake, your stressful thoughts begin, and you cannot get back to sleep.

What can I do about my sleep problems?

Each of these types of sleep disturbance can be influenced by racing thoughts. These thoughts are usually of a stressful nature. They increase your nervous system arousal, making it difficult to get any rest. It is easy for these stressful thoughts to flood your mind because there is nothing happening during the night hours to distract you from them. During the day, you can often push these thoughts aside because you have other things to focus on. However, at night, there is nothing to grab your attention.

Here is a series of simple steps that should help you have a better night's sleep.

	Simple sleep strategy
1.	In the evening, avoid caffeine and sugary drinks and food.
2.	In the lead up to your bedtime, start to wind down. Turn off stimulating television or stop engaging in other activities around the house that cause you to feel more alert.
3.	Have a small snack rich in carbohydrates.
4.	Get into a comfortable bed and into a comfortable position. Slow your breathing. Relax your muscle tension.
5.	Give your mind something to think about that is not emotionally arousing. This could be writing a simple story in your head, listing in your mind all the countries you can think of, starting with A, then B, etc. Count backwards by 7s from a randomly selected number.
6.	If your thoughts drift to more stressful thoughts, acknowledge that is what is happening then return to the activity you chose to keep your mind focused.
7.	Allow yourself to drift off to sleep.

Exercise available at elemen.com.au

The goal here is to create the right sort of internal environment to facilitate a good night's sleep. Avoid caffeine and sugary food or drinks because they can have a stimulating effect on your nervous system. In general, you should be aiming to 'turn off' by reducing the number of external stimulating activities. You do these things in preparation for sleep.

Carbohydrates can also increase your readiness for sleep. This is because carbohydrates contribute to an increase in your brain of a protein called tryptophan. This is a building block for a neurotransmitter called serotonin and a hormone called melatonin. Serotonin has a role in controlling sleep, appetite and mood. Melatonin release is triggered by darkness, and this hormone helps promote a regular sleep-wake cycle. This process, triggered by eating a carbohydrate-rich snack before bedtime, helps you sleep.

When your mind is already overrun by thoughts that are keeping you awake, it seems counterintuitive to give your brain something else to think about. However, it is not the thoughts themselves that will keep you awake. It is the nature of the thoughts that will have an effect on your sleep. In this way, you want to distract yourself from thinking stress-related thoughts, replacing them with thoughts that will not cause you to react emotionally. You should aim to keep your brain busy with mundane thoughts so that your mind is distracted from the stress-inducing thoughts. We like to refer to this activity as 'busy work' for your brain. It is the modern-day equivalent of counting sheep.

Mundane thoughts will allow you to drift off to sleep whereas stress-related thoughts will keep you alert and awake. Your brain is always active so it is not possible to stop thinking. When you think of things that cause your nervous system to respond by increasing your arousal, you will have trouble sleeping. If you think calming or even boring thoughts, your brain will trigger the processes that lead you to falling asleep.

The same strategy of giving your mind something other than stressful things to think about can be applied if you awaken during the night. Simply get settled and focus on the mundane thoughts you have selected, allowing yourself to drift off back to sleep.

Expectations, demands and preferences

In an upcoming section, we will be discussing how your thinking can affect how you feel and the choices you make about what you are going to do about the problems in life you face. Here, we want to introduce you to the idea that the rules you set for yourself can influence how you feel. Also, we will consider how you can enforce those rules in ways that make things more stressful for you rather than less stressful.

Setting expectations

The expectations you set for yourself can be unreasonable. You can make the mistaken assumption that if you just try hard enough, you will be able to cope with whatever comes your way. So, you just push yourself harder and harder, expecting that you will cope. We will be talking about coping later. Here, we want to talk about the rules you set for yourself and your expectations for how you will be able to live by those rules.

There are two features of the expectations you can set for yourself that will present you with problems. Firstly, it is easy to set expectations and standards for your behaviour that would exceed most people's capacity to cope. The rules you set for yourself may include aspects such as 'I should do everything I set out to do', 'I should do everything properly and well' and 'I have no choice but to do everything I have to do'.

Secondly, these rules you make tend to be set in stone. That is, no matter what is happening in your life, you believe that you have to rigidly adhere to these rules. You can believe this to be true even if the demands on you exceed your normal coping capacity. You can believe it to be true even if you also hold the view that others should not have to deal with such a huge demand. After all, we are all quite capable of having a different set of rules for ourselves than we have for others. We expect ourselves to cope when we are more sympathetic towards others in the same situation.

In an effort to start to bring your situation under control, you must consider the expectations you are setting for yourself. The rules you set need to be flexible so that you can adjust when the demands on you fluctuate. Below are some commonsense reminders you might like to consider.

1.	There are only so many hours in the day, and there is only so much you can do during those hours. Expecting yourself to do more and more in your available time is unrealistic.
2.	Having more things to attend to than is usual means that you may not be able to do them all to the high standard you would normally apply.
3.	All you can do is the best that you can do. That might mean that you cannot do everything with 100% efficiency. If you are functioning at, say, 60% of your normal way of coping, it is unrealistic to expect that you can still function at 100% capacity. Just aim to do the best you can on any given day. If 60% is the best you can do, then 60% is acceptable.
4.	Everyone has a limit. If there is too much to do or too many stressful things have happened, it is not surprising that you feel your limit has been reached. Be aware of this and learn to adjust and adapt to the changed circumstances you are experiencing.
5.	Even if things feel like they will continue to be as stressful as they are today, you can learn ways to manage your time differently, cope more effectively, and deal with how stressed you feel. The feeling of being overwhelmed can be controlled and will pass.

Before moving on to learning how to manage your time in a more effective way, in an effort to feel less overwhelmed, we need to consider one other factor in relation to expectations. This relates to a simple mistake that people make that tends to increase how overwhelmed you feel rather than relieves it.

Language you use when talking to yourself

One of the problems that you can create for yourself is that stressful things happening in your life can feel worse because of the way you talk to yourself about your experiences. The expectations you set can feel more exaggerated because of the way you view them.

In particular, we are all capable of making demands on ourselves, even when they do not exist. When we talk to ourselves, we say things like "I must do this" and "I should do that" or "I have to do what I set out to do". Everyone does this and, usually, it does not have any really noticeable effect on how we are feeling. However, when we feel stressed or overwhelmed, talking like this exacerbates the stress we are feeling.

Consider the example below of Lydia and her busy day.

> *Lydia was standing in her kitchen, holding a cup of coffee. It was early, and the children were not yet awake. She was thinking about all the things she had to do. She knew she must get started in getting the children's breakfast ready and their school lunches organised. She knew that she had to get them to school in time for them to catch up with their friends before class started. She thought she should have arranged to have her car serviced and made a mental note that she must do that next week or sometime when she had a minute. Her thoughts then turned to work. She thought she absolutely had to get onto the problem that had arisen between two employees, and she thought that she should do that first thing this morning. She thought of all the other things she had to do at work today. She had a report she had to finish and some tasks she had to do because they had been hanging around for a couple of days. There were phone calls she absolutely had to get around to. She also thought she really had to remember to make an appointment for the children to have their hair cut. She chastised herself for not having done it sooner. Lydia then thought that she had to spend more time with her elderly parents and that she should do more for them than she was already doing. She wondered where she would find the time to do that. She decided that she would just have to find the time. Lydia knew that she had to contact a friend she had had a disagreement with to sort out the issues they were having. Their disagreement had been going on for too long, and she really should have fixed things with her. Lydia sighed. The day had barely started, and she already felt overwhelmed.*

Lydia's self-talk was full of 'must', 'should' and 'have to'. With language like that going through her mind, everything seemed like a pressure. We all do this. We feel like things are imperative, so we make demands of ourselves. Even without really noticing, we speak to ourselves in ways that exacerbate our stress. It makes us feel that we have no choice, and this perceived lack of choice is stressful in itself.

But, is this really true? It is actually the case that you could lay on the grass and look at the sky all day long if that is what you chose to do. Of course, you probably would not do that but you absolutely could do that if you chose to do that.

In fact, most, if not all, of what we do is a choice we make. We may feel some pressure to do things or to act in a particular way, but the way we act is based on decisions we make for ourselves. We take into account all of the information available to us at the time, and then we make a decision about what we are going to do.

Are you unsure this is true? Think about it. How many times have you acted in a particular way or undertaken a particular task because it suits you to do that, even if the task you undertake is not a preferred one? Consider the following comments.

> I will do it to get it out of the way.
>
> I will do it so she stops nagging me about it.

> I will make a dental appointment even though I hate the dentist because I want to make sure my teeth are healthy.
>
> If I get the housework out of the way, the rest of the day is mine to do what I want.
>
> I would rather do the job myself than leave it to my colleague.
>
> It is easier to pick up after the children than to keep growling at them.

You can probably generate a long list of similar comments you make to yourself. All reflect the choices we make and the decisions we reach. These choices generally have good underlying rationales. We make these choices and decisions because, in some way, they work for us.

Then why do we keep talking to ourselves like things are imperative and the demands are real? There are probably numerous reasons. We might do it because it has become a habit. We might do it because it feels like it is true. We might do it because of the stress we feel. But what would happen if you stopped making these demands and, instead, expressed them as preferences in a way that is genuinely the case?

Reframe your expectations in terms of preferences not demands

To alleviate the additional stress that is caused by using demanding language, you might like to try changing the way you speak to yourself. To start to understand how to do this, let's revisit Lydia's early morning thoughts.

> *Lydia was standing in her kitchen, holding a cup of coffee. It was early, and the children were not yet awake. She was thinking about all the things she wanted to do. She thought she would like to get started soon to get the children's breakfast underway and their school lunches packed. She decided she would head off with enough time for the children to catch up with their friends before classes because she knew that was what they liked to do. She reminded herself that, when she found a moment, she would book her car in for a service because she liked to keep on top of those sorts of things. Her thoughts then turned to work. She decided that today was the day she would sort out the difficulties that had arisen between two employees. She chose to do that as her first work task of the day so that she could get it out of the way. She thought of all the other things she wanted to do at work today. She had a report she wanted to finish and tasks she would prefer to get done because they had been hanging around for a couple of days. There were phone calls she wanted to make, so she decided to fit those calls around the other things she wanted to get done. Thinking about fitting things in, Lydia thought she would find a moment to make an appointment for the children to have their hair cut. She thought she probably could have done this sooner but accepted there were other things that had taken her attention. Lydia then thought about wanting to spend more time with her elderly parents and do more for them. She decided this was important enough to her that she would*

> *choose to rearrange her time so that she could manage to do this. Lydia also thought about wanting to fix things with her friend with whom she had had a disagreement. She thought she preferred to do this rather than let things drag on. Lydia put down her coffee cup. She was at the start of the day, and she had a clear idea of what she was going to choose to do.*

Do not underestimate the additional stress you can feel from wording things in a demanding way. It is a good idea to practice changing your demanding internal self-talk into a statement of preference. Consider the following examples.

Reframing demanding self-talk - examples	
Demand	Preference
I must cook dinner.	*I think I will get on and cook dinner; otherwise, I will end up with a house full of hungry people... including me.*
I should go and talk to the manager about all the in-fighting in the department even though I don't want to.	*I think I will go and talk to the manager about all the in-fighting in the department. I would rather not have to do that but it would be good to hand the problem on to someone who can do something about it.*
I have to go to work early to get everything done.	*I will choose to go to work early so that I can get things done and out of the way, That would be a relief.*
I should phone my mother.	*I think I will phone my mother. That will make her happy.*

Below is a worksheet you can use. Catch yourself making demands and reframe them as a statement of preference.

Reframing demanding self-talk	
Demand	Preference

Worksheet available at elemen.com.au

Before going on to consider other ways our self-talk can influence how you feel, it is worth examining techniques to manage your time in a way that will reduce that overwhelming feeling that comes with too many stressful things happening in your life.

Reprioritising and managing your time

One of the problems you face when you have too many things to do or are overwhelmed by too many stressful things is that it feels like there is never enough time available to do all you have to do. As a result, it is worth considering some time management strategies.

Let's start by considering the list of things you need to do. We can work out ways to approach this list.

Prioritise what you need to do

People often make long lists of things to do with the intention of crossing items off as they are completed. Long lists of things can seem daunting. However, not everything on your list of things to do is of equal importance. We do not always take this into consideration when we are trying to get things done. You can, in effect, end up wasting time doing unimportant things when much more important things are waiting for your attention.

When you make a list of the things you feel you need to do, divide the items into:

> *Important items:* These are the things you must get done most urgently or urgently need your attention.

> *Somewhat important items:* These are things that you will need to get around to doing within a reasonable amount of time.

> *Unimportant or less important items:* These are things that could be left as it does not really matter if they are done or when they are done.

You should aim to do the important items first, followed by the somewhat important items and, finally, the unimportant items if you have time to get around to them. Let's look at an example of a list of things to do that has been re-prioritised in this way.

We can look at the list of a person, Kelly, who is facing a few major things. In this case, let's consider someone who is dealing with settling their mother's estate after her death, dealing with her son Ben's health problems, and dealing with being busy at work. We can start by looking at this person's list of things to do.

Kelly's list of things to do	
1.	Meet with the lawyer about Mum's estate.
2.	Get together the documents the lawyer wants.
3.	Take Ben to have some blood tests.
4.	Arrange for a specialist's appointment for Ben.
5.	Go to the supermarket.
6.	Clean out the linen cupboard.
7.	Finish the report at work.
8.	Arrange a meeting to discuss the next project at work.
9.	Update contact list at work.
10.	Meet with stakeholders about possible outcomes of the current project.
11.	Pay the phone bill.
12.	Replace the annoying tap in the laundry.
13.	Reorganise the pantry.
14.	Teach Ben to monitor his own blood sugar levels.
15.	Reassign duties to take advantage of workers' expertise and take into account their preferences.
16.	Return best friend's message.

Now, we can prioritise these things that Kelly has put on her list. We can do this by dividing the list into three lists based on the importance of each item.

Prioritisation of things to do - example		
Highly important	Moderately important	Less important
Take Ben to have some blood tests. *Arrange for a specialist's appointment for Ben.* *Teach Ben to monitor his own blood sugar levels.*	*Get together the documents the lawyer wants.* *Meet with the lawyer about Mum's estate.* *Finish the report at work.* *Arrange a meeting to discuss the next project at work.* *Meet with stakeholders about possible outcomes of the current project.* *Go to the supermarket.* *Pay the phone bill.*	*Clean out the linen cupboard.* *Update contact list at work.* *Replace the annoying tap in the laundry.* *Reorganise the pantry.* *Reassign duties to take advantage of workers' expertise and take into account their preferences.* *Return best friend's message.*

In this new, re-jigged list of things to do, Kelly has three highly important things to do. They all relate to Ben's health and they are all relatively easily achieved. One involves a phone call, one requires that she take Ben to have a blood test after school, and the last one involves sitting down with Ben in the evening and explaining to him what he needs to do to look after his own health. Once these things are done, Kelly can move on to her next list.

Although the 'moderately important' list looks longer, it largely relates to three things. There are tasks that Kelly will have to get onto soon regarding her mother's estate. These relate to getting the documents together and then making an appointment to speak with the lawyer. Then there are tasks Kelly will need to do soon for work. She needs to finish a report she has started and arrange two meetings. The other tasks relate to the smooth running of her household, which will have an impact on others if she does not get around to them.

The last list relates to items that are on Kelly's wish list but there will be no real consequence if she takes a while to get around to them. Although there might be advantages in getting them done, there is no real urgency for these things to happen.

Below is a prioritisation list worksheet you can use to sort out the things you have to do in terms of their importance or urgency.

Prioritisation of things to do		
Highly important	Moderately important	Less important

Worksheet available at elemen.com.au

Break down your high priority, important tasks

Sometimes, items on these lists can still seem overwhelming. You may tend to avoid doing them by filling in your time with less important tasks just because the important items feel too difficult. One way to overcome this is to break the items into more manageable steps. Each of these steps can seem less overwhelming. If you work through the steps, you end up achieving your goal of completing the important item.

Consider the following example.

Examples of steps to complete an important task	
Task to be completed	*Sorting out Mum's estate*
Steps	*Make a list of the documents I need so that I can be sure I have them all.*
	Go through the file boxes of papers from Mum's house and pull out the documents I need.
	Put the documents in an organised file in the order outlined on the list of documents I wrote up.
	Phone the lawyer's office for an appointment.
	Attend appointment with lawyer, taking the file of documents with me.

Avoid distractions and deals

It is an easy trap to fall into to avoid doing the important things by allowing yourself to be distracted. These distractions usually are of less importance than the task you identified as of high importance. Remember to complete the most important tasks before moving on to less important tasks.

It is also a form of avoidance to make deals with yourself, such as, "I will look through the boxes of documents after I have dusted the bookcase". These deals are designed to make it acceptable to not do the important thing you have identified you will do but least want to do. Of course, even if you do undertake a less important activity, the most important one still remains.

How to make time when you seem to have none

When you start learning time management techniques, it can seem impossible. In particular, it seems inconceivable that you can make time when none seems to be available. It feels like there are not enough hours in the day to do all you need. However, it is possible to make time if you follow some rules.

There are four 'must do' rules for making time. These include:

Learn to say no.

> Even when you are overwhelmed, and people understand this, you can still be asked to do more. It is all right for you to put your needs over those of other people's less important needs. You can do this even if you are the sort of person who would normally want to be of assistance to others. It just takes an understanding that sometimes your needs are greater than the needs of another person. In fact, it is not possible for it to be any other way. Just ask yourself, "Whose need is most important?". When you learn to comfortably say no, you can find extra time that you would normally devote to unnecessarily doing things for other people.

Ignore the unimportant items on your to-do list.

> These items on your to-do list should only come to your attention if you have completed all of your important and somewhat important tasks. Remember, they are rated as unimportant because they can be left without any undue concern. Indeed, these are the sorts of tasks that can be handed on to other people to do. In an understanding of the demands on you, your family and friends may ask if they can help you. Learn to feel comfortable handing on unimportant tasks when these offers are made. This will buy you more time, and it will help the people who genuinely care about you feel that they are doing something useful to assist you.

Make reasonable time estimates.

When you are working out how long it will take you to do things, try to make a realistic estimate of how long each task will take. Things typically take longer than you think because when we make an estimate, we do not take into account interruptions or events we do not expect. So, do not try to squash into the day as many tasks as you can in the shortest period of time. If you do this, you will become increasingly frantic and frustrated at not getting everything done, and these feelings tend to interfere with your productivity. Usually, you can do more if you pace yourself well and remain focused.

Build relaxation time into your schedule.

For the very reason that you make more progress if you approach your tasks in a paced way, you should build into your day rest times when you can relax. Frantically moving from one task to the next will exhaust you and slow you down as the day progresses. You would be better off setting aside rest times that should only be interrupted by emergencies.

There are other rules you can follow if you choose. These are not necessary but may help you manage your time better and produce time when none seems to be available.

Consider the following options and identify those you might try to use.

	Possible time generating ideas
	Generate a short list of brief tasks (5 minutes) that you can do while you are waiting for something else to occur or if you find yourself with a few moments before you start your next important task. Consider these to be fill-in tasks.
	Learn to multitask. You can think about doing one thing while you do another.
	Hand on your unimportant tasks to others.
	Do an additional task while you are watching television. For example, you can watch television and fold the clean laundry.
	Stop using avoidance and distraction strategies when you are faced with an important task.
	Time-limit activities that are not productive when there are important tasks to do. For example, talk to your friend when they telephone you, but not for half an hour.

	Put things back in their place as soon as you have finished with them. That is, do not leave things lying around. You will just have to find time to put them away later when the task of putting away multiple things will seem like a bigger one.
	Turn your back on perfectionism. You have to get things done. These things do not have to be done absolutely perfectly.

Checklist available at elemen.com.au

When you are overwhelmed by too many demanding pressures on your time, it is important to adopt good time management techniques. These techniques allow you to structure your day in a more effective way and to work as efficiently as possible. However, time management is not the only thing you need to consider when you are overwhelmed by too much to do and too many burdens. Next, let's look at the problem from a different perspective.

Changing your thinking

To feel better, you might have to change the way you view the circumstances in your life in an effort to alter the way you react to them. Certain ways of thinking tend to make us feel more distressed, more vulnerable and more overwhelmed than we need to feel. The goal is to challenge this type of unhelpful thinking so that it can be replaced with the type of thinking that is a more accurate reflection of your situation. Let's consider ways you can challenge unhelpful thinking and replace it with the types of thoughts that allow you to see things more clearly and choose behaviours that will help you.

How are our thoughts affected?

As we go through life, we can develop unhelpful thinking styles or errors in our thinking. These errors influence how we interpret the world around us and how we fit into that world. In an attempt to make sense of the world, we develop 'templates' or models of how we think things should work.

For example, you might develop a template that tells you that you have to be the best at everything you do. On the surface, this seems workable. You may just have to work hard and keep things in your control. However, if you have a template that you *have* to be the best, what happens when you have too much to do and too little time to do it? You then become upset with yourself. You feel like you are not good enough, even in situations where you tried your hardest to succeed. We have met lots of people who want to succeed, but because of factors outside their control, they have been unable to achieve the standard of perfection they set. This may be you. Unfortunately, your template might tell you that to be 'good enough', you *must* be the best in all areas of your life, that you must function at 100% capacity no matter what, and that if you do not do something perfectly, you have failed. You can see the problem.

Our individual templates are put together based on information from a variety of sources, including, for example, our personality and our experiences throughout life. If the messages we receive from our experiences in life are good and healthy ones, we tend to have good and healthy templates of how the world works and how we fit into that world. However, if the messages are distorted in some way (e.g., being told you have to be the best at everything you do, that no one will like you if you disagree with them, your needs are not as important as other people's needs), then the template we develop will reflect these messages and will be unhelpful.

Core beliefs

So, how does this template affect us? It tells us how we should respond when dealing with our world and the people in it. The information we gather determines our 'core beliefs' about three things:

How safe or dangerous we perceive the world to be.

Our place in that world and our value as a person.

How certain the future feels.

These core beliefs are not the 'truth' of things. They develop as a result of the information we gather along the way in life, whether or not that information is helpful or unhelpful, clear or confusing, or accurate or distorted.

If we have helpful, clear and accurate templates, then our core beliefs are healthy, and our thinking does not contain errors about how the world works and how we fit into that world. However, if we have unhelpful, confusing and distorted templates, our thinking contains errors that affect how we react to the world and how we view ourselves in that world.

Cognitive errors

Cognitive errors are the errors in thinking that occur when our templates of how the world works and how we fit into that world send us the wrong message. Our thinking about our experiences is then altered by the wrong message. Problems arise when we engage in certain types of cognitive errors.

Below are some of the most common cognitive errors. As you read through them, think about whether these types of errors occur in your thinking.

Table 3: Descriptions of the common errors in thinking.

Types of errors in thinking	
Error type	*Error in thinking*
Filtering	A person whose thinking is affected by filtering takes the negative details of an event and exaggerates them while filtering out any positive aspects of the situation. For example, you might berate yourself for not getting everything done but ignore the fact that you had a productive day getting lots of things completed.
Polarised thinking	With polarised thinking, things are either 'black or white' or 'all or nothing'. People who think this way place situations in 'either/or' categories, with no middle ground to account for the complexity of most situations. For example, you might think you have to be able to cope with an excessive workload, or you are completely hopeless.

Overgeneralisation	A person makes a conclusion based on one event or a single piece of information. In this way, if something bad happens to them on one occasion, they expect it to happen over and over again. For example, you might make an error because of the excessive demands being placed on you so then you believe that you cannot be trusted to do anything properly.
Jumping to conclusions	If a person jumps to conclusions, they 'know' what the other person is thinking about without that person saying so. For example, just because you are feeling overwhelmed and unable to cope, you start to think that your manager is disappointed in you.
Catastrophising	A person who catastrophises expects disaster to strike, no matter what. A person hears about a problem and uses *what-if* questions to imagine the worst outcome. For example, because you are struggling with excessive demands, you start to worry that your partner will leave you or your manager will fire you.
Personalisation	A person believes that everything others do or say is some kind of direct, personal reaction to them. They take everything personally. For example, your friend makes a comment about the amount of time stay-at-home mothers get to spend with their children, and you believe she is criticising you for having to work.
Control fallacies	This occurs when a person strongly endorses the view that they must be in control of all situations. This can occur in two ways. Firstly, there is external control, where the person feels they are a helpless victim of fate, and secondly, internal control, where a person assumes responsibility for the pain and unhappiness of others. For example, your manager arranges for a more equitable distribution of workload. Your colleagues are unhappy they have to do more, so you believe you are responsible for their unhappiness because you complained about your excessive workload.
Fallacy of fairness	A person who believes they know what is fair will feel resentful and unhappy if others disagree with them. People who judge every event in their lives in terms of whether or not it is fair will often feel resentful, angry and hopeless. For example, you feel resentful because you have had to deal with so many problems when other family members have not been burdened by these types of things.

Blaming	This person holds other people responsible for their own emotional pain. Alternatively, they may blame themselves for every problem – even those clearly outside their control. For example, you tell yourself that if only you had forced yourself to take on even more work when your colleague resigned, management would not have hired the person that the rest of your colleagues dislike
Shoulds	Should statements (e.g., I should visit my parents more) are made by people who hold rigid rules about how the world should work and how everyone should behave. Breaking these rules makes a person angry. They also feel guilty when they violate their own rules. For example, you tell yourself you should be handling all the things you are facing even though your friends say they are amazed you are doing as much as you are at the moment.
Emotional reasoning	People with this distortion in thinking are guided by what they 'feel' is the truth. They will rely on their feelings to establish whether or not something is 'fact'. If a person feels stupid and boring, then they must be stupid and boring. Emotional reasoning blocks rationality and logic. For example, you believe you are worthless because you are struggling to cope with excessive demands.
Fallacy of change	A person with this type of thinking will believe that if they apply enough pressure, others will change to meet their needs. This person needs others to change because they cannot cope if others disagree with them or behave in ways that are contrary to how this person feels they should behave. For example, you believe that if you complain to your partner enough about how much you have to do, they will see that they should change their ways and help more even though you do not directly ask them for that help.
Global labelling	A person generalises a small number of features or characteristics of themselves or others and inflates them into a global statement or judgment. This goes beyond overgeneralising. Rather than take into account the context of a situation, the person will apply this judgment to all aspects of a person or situation. For example, you might label yourself as a 'hopeless coper' just because you are struggling to cope at the moment.

Always being right	When a person engages in this error of thinking, they insist that all views held by them or actions done by them are correct. In their view, they cannot make a mistake or be misinformed. For example, if you hold the view that you should always be able to cope with anything that comes your way and you believe you are right about everything, it would be hard to admit you need help. You are more likely to just keep trying harder and harder until it becomes impossible to deal with what you are facing.
Heaven's reward fallacy	A person who engages in this type of thinking believes that a person's hard work and sacrifice will pay off in the end, as if someone is keeping track of what everyone does in life. Sharing some similarities with the fallacy of fairness thinking, this person believes that the one who does the most or, works the hardest or sacrifices the most will be the person who is rewarded at some point in the future. For example, you might tell yourself that if you keep taking on more and more without complaining, then there will be some sort of benefit coming your way from all your efforts.

Let's consider how these errors in thinking affect a person's point of view. Below are examples of these types of logical errors in thinking, along with a more rational point of view.

Table 4: *Examples of rational and irrational perspectives for each error in thinking.*

Correcting your thinking	
Error in thinking	*A rational view*
Filtering	
Joel's boss praised him for his hard work and pointed out that his colleagues had nice things to say about how much Joe had helped them. He also said that Joel needed to bring some stocktaking records up to date. Joel only focused on the boss' mention of the stocktaking records. He concluded his boss is unhappy with his performance.	In general, Joel should be pleased with his performance. He received recognition for the many things he had done well, with only one issue being raised that required more attention. It would have been appropriate for Joe to look at his situation and say that, overall, the evidence showed that he was doing a good job.

Polarised thinking	
Stuart was studying engineering at uni. He was also working long hours in a casual job to pay the bills. He was barely managing to cope with the demands on him. Towards the end of his semester at uni, Stuart had three big assignments due to be submitted in the same week. Stuart was overloaded, he was not sleeping enough, and he felt stressed and generally ill. He realised he was not coping. Stuart berated himself for being completely hopeless because he was struggling to complete the assignments and maintain all the other things he needed to do in his life.	Stuart should have considered his struggle to cope in the context of the overall demands on his time and his general performance. In reality, Stuart was already overloaded, and then he was faced with considerable extra challenges. It was not reasonable for Stuart to view himself as hopeless. He had been managing a huge workload for a long time and had done so reasonably successfully. It was only when he was faced with a significant increase in his workload that he had trouble coping. It was not the case that he either could easily do the work or he was hopeless, as Stuart believed. It was more a case that it was understandable that Stuart was going to struggle when he was given significantly more to do. After all, he was already stretched to the limit.

Overgeneralisation	
When her supervisor went on leave, Sophie was asked to cover that person's job as well as maintaining the work in her own position. Although it was a challenge to do this, Sophie managed to complete all the work required of her for a number of weeks. In the final week of her double duties, Sophie made an error, sending an email that contained sensitive information to the wrong recipient. When she became aware of what she had done, Sophie was distraught. She formed the view that this error proved that she was untrustworthy and incapable of adequately doing the work being asked of her. Although her boss was understanding, Sophie thought she could never be trusted again and offered to resign.	Sophie would have been better off considering that one error when she was faced with an overwhelming amount of work did not reflect a general level of incompetence. She could have viewed this error as a reflection of the fact that she was being asked to do the work of two full-time positions, and this would have increased the likelihood of an error, no matter who was placed in that position. Further, the error did not really reflect an error in judgment on her part. Rather, it was a function of the fact that she had too much to do without enough time to do them.

Jumping to conclusions	
Rebecca's boss asked her to take on a special project in addition to her normal day-to-day workload. This special project required her to learn new skills. There was no one in the organisation who could teach her these skills, so she had to look to other sources on the Internet to learn how to do what was being asked of her. This made the task very difficult. In addition, she had little time to devote to learning these new skills. Her boss was understanding and asked that she just do her best. Rebecca was struggling to cope. She found it difficult to learn how to even start the new project and it just felt so overwhelming. She felt that her boss must be disappointed in her performance and consider her to be not up to the task.	Rather than jumping to the conclusion that her boss was disappointed in her performance and viewed her as incompetent, Rebecca should have focused on the objective facts. Her boss gave her the project on the understanding that no one in the organisation had the skills needed to complete it and that she would have to teach herself the needed skills. Further, her boss had clearly stated that he understood the task was a difficult one and asked only that she try her best and do what she could under difficult circumstances. These facts pointed to Rebecca's boss being more sympathetic with regard to the challenge she faced than she was willing to be for herself.

Catastrophising	
Patricia had been facing enormous pressure in her life. She was excessively busy at work, her husband was ill and her children and her parents needed her assistance. As a result, Patricia forget her friend's birthday. Usually, she sent a card and flowers to her friend but this year she simply forgot. Patricia thought her friend would never forgive her and would never speak to her again, despite the fact that they had been friends for many years and her friend was a very understanding person.	Patricia formed a view about what would happen as a consequence of her failure to remember her friend's birthday that was completely inconsistent with what she knew about her friend. Given that their friendship had endured for many years and given that her friend was known to be understanding, the chances were very slim that her friend would be so hurt by Patricia's mistake that their friendship would fail. Patricia was reacting to her own emotional response to her failing to remember her friend's birthday rather than predicting a likely future. In any case, Patricia would not know how her friend had responded until she spoke with her friend about the matter. Predicting a terrible future does not increase the chances that a terrible future will happen, especially if the prediction is based on incorrect information.
Personalisation	
Julia was talking to a friend about how busy and stressed she has been. She complained about the demands of work and the challenges of balancing her time between work and her home with her husband and children. Julia's friend made a comment about how different her own life was to Julia's. She said that most of her time was spent caring for her children. Although it was not her friend's intention, Julia interpreted this comment as a criticism of her decision to be a working mother. Her feelings were hurt.	Julia made the mistake of assigning meaning to her friend's comments that was not intended. Rather than seeing the statement as an observation about the differences in people's lives, Julia took the statement personally and responded emotionally to this interpretation. If she had been able to see that it was a statement of truth that people had different types of demands in their lives, Julia would not have taken the statement personally and would not have had her feelings hurt.

Control fallacies	
Ben arrived home from work after another stressful day. He was exhausted. When he got home, Ben's wife was agitated. An argument had developed between his wife and a colleague and she had brought her bad mood home with her. She was irritated and did not ask Ben about his day. Despite her mentioning the argument, Ben interpreted his wife's mood as her being angry with him. He asked her what he had done to make her so annoyed.	Ben had fallen into the trap of thinking that if only he had behaved differently, everything would have turned out differently. Ben ignored the obvious external contributors to his wife's stress and felt that her unhappiness was something he should have been able to control by behaving differently. Ben should have recognised that there was nothing he could have done to control what happened in his wife's workplace. In fact, he probably made his own and his wife's stress worse by making the problem all about him.
Fallacy of fairness	
Jonathan had been asked to fill a position at work until the job could be advertised. He knew that he did not have the qualifications needed for the job but his supervisor had offered him lots of support during the time he was acting in the role. Despite knowing he did not have the qualifications, Jonathan applied for the job anyway. However, he was angry and upset when the job was given to a more qualified candidate. He thought it was unfair that someone who had never done the job before was given the position.	Despite your best efforts, sometimes things do not work out the way you would like. Someone more qualified may come along, and sometimes, you do not get what you think you deserve. Jonathan rejected all the information that contradicted his point of view that if he did a good job and acted in the position, he would be given the job as a matter of fairness. Things did not work out the way he had expected, and he was disappointed. His disappointment had nothing to do with unfairness, but with the fact that he wanted something he did not end up getting. He would have been better off realising that his employer was seeking someone with particular qualifications, so it was reasonable that such a person would end up getting the job.

Blaming	
Jack was offered the job he had been doing for a couple of months, filling in for his supervisor. His supervisor was not returning and Jack had the opportunity to have this promotion. But the demands of this job were great and he did not like the work as it took him away from his preferred, hands-on approach with customers. Therefore, he said no. Now the job position has been filled by someone his colleagues do not like. They consider him to be an authoritarian supervisor who does not have the skills to form good working relationship with employees. Jack has been wracked with guilt, blaming himself for his co-workers' unhappiness. He said that if only he had taken the job he did not want, none of these problems would have occurred.	Although it was up to Jack whether or not he accepted the offered position, anything beyond that was not in his control. He cannot be blamed or blame himself for decisions made by an interview panel when he was not a member of that panel. Although he might be disappointed with the outcome, this is not the same thing as being to blame for what happened.

Shoulds	
Craig's friends could see that he was not coping with all the demands he was facing. He was very stressed at work. He was a single dad of two young children. He did a lot of community work. However, Craig felt he was not doing a good enough job. His friends reassured him that was not the case. They told him that they could not do what he did every day. They saw him as an inspiration. Craig liked to do everything well… perfectly. He felt he should be doing more to show he was a worthwhile person. He set very high standards for himself. Despite reaching his limit, he told himself that he should do more and must do better.	Craig has a list of things he should or must do. The rules he set for himself are very rigid. He has to do things perfectly; he should do more. Craig needs rules that will provide him with some flexibility that can take into account the current demands on him and the normal fluctuations in his ability to cope with the demands being placed on him.

Emotional reasoning	
Suzanne was struggling to cope with all the demands she was facing. She was a working mother whose partner worked away from home for weeks at a time. Her father recently experienced heart problems and her mother needed her help. She found herself running between work, home, her parents' home, and taking her father to his medical appointments. She was doing the best she could and others reassured her that she could not expect more of herself. Suzanne's busy life was making her feel anxious. Her nervous system was revved up and she could not sleep. As a result of feeling anxious, Suzanne reached the conclusion that she was worthless and was failing as a wife, mother, daughter and employee.	Suzanne has this the wrong way around. She has a strong emotional reaction to the pressures on her, and this has caused her to conclude that she is worthless. This was despite all that she was managing to achieve under difficult circumstances. So, her emotional reaction was causing her to form a negative view of herself. Instead, she should have considered how her demanding life should have influenced how she reacted to her situation, not the other way around.
Fallacy of change	
Lisa felt overwhelmed. Both she and her husband, Adrian, worked full-time in busy jobs but Lisa was the person who was doing all the housework, looking after the children and doing all the shopping and cooking. Lisa kept complaining to Adrian that it was too much for her to do. Adrian did not seem to be listening. Lisa believed that if she complained enough, Adrian would see that she needed more help and would change his behaviour and do more. Adrian seemed oblivious to her complaints. Increasingly, Lisa felt angry and resentful. She believed that Adrian should realise what she needed and take it upon himself to change his behaviour.	Lisa made the mistake of assuming that her complaints would encourage Adrian to be more aware and insightful. However, her belief that Adrian should 'know better' and take it upon himself to change was getting her nowhere. Instead, Lisa should have clearly communicated what she needed from him. By assertively stating what she needed, Lisa would be taking control of her own situation rather than waiting for Adrian to 'get the hint'.

Global labelling

Throughout his life, Brad had coped pretty well with things. Despite having a busy life, he seemed to manage well. However, recently, things had overwhelmed Brad. The demands at work had increased and there were other pressures in his life. In addition, Brad had not been very well, taking some time to recover from a virus and this was slowing him down. Brad started criticising himself and he formed the view that he was terrible at coping with life demands. He thought everyone else did a better job at coping. He thought he just could not do what was expected of him.	The fact that Brad is struggling to cope at the moment has caused him to form the view that he is terrible at coping with life demands in a global sense. Brad would have been better off taking into account his coping history, which was good. Further, he should have recognised that there were particular challenges at the moment that were contributing to him feeling like things were overwhelming him. This would have allowed him to recognise that his problem was more related to his life circumstances rather than it reflecting a flaw in him.

Always being right

Ian had always prided himself on being able to cope with a heavy workload and many life demands. But lately, things had gotten on top of him. He had taken on too much at work and this had caused him to have to work long hours. He was not getting enough sleep and had too little time to do the sorts of things that would normally help him cope, such as exercise. Ian needed help, and help would have been available to him had he asked for it. But Ian held the view that he was right about everything. He believed he was a good coper and, because he was always right, he believed he had to cope well in all situations. As a result, Ian refused to ask for the help he obviously needed.	Ian's need to always be right was causing him a problem. It was blinding him to the fact that our ability to cope fluctuates depending on what is happening in our life. He would have been better off accepting that all people need help some of the time. This would have made it easier for him to ask for the help he needed and take advantage of the help that was available.

Heaven's reward fallacy	
Chloe knew she was under pressure. She felt stressed all the time, was not sleeping well and could not concentrate. But she did not say anything. In fact, every time she was asked to do more, she agreed. She never complained even though she was suffering. Chloe believed that if she kept doing everything that was asked of her, no matter how difficult it was for her, there would be a payoff in the end. She believed that something good would happen because she had been so obliging.	The trouble with Chloe's view that all her hard work would pay off in the end is that there was no one keeping a record of what she was doing. While she kept doing what others asked her to do, they just formed an expectation that she would continue to do so. They were not considering the effect on her of the demands they were making on her. Chloe would have been better off taking charge of what she was willing to do and considering her own needs because no one else was paying attention. Learning to say no at times when she was already overloaded would create a situation where she had better control of her own stress levels.

It is apparent that these types of logical errors do not make things easy for us. Quite the opposite. They lead us to misinterpret events so that we adopt a limited or negative perspective that colours how we view things, our emotional responses, and the choices of how we behave as a consequence.

Why do we think in unhelpful ways?

Why do we think in ways that are distorted and not particularly helpful? To understand why errors in thinking happen, we have to consider the theory behind cognitive behaviour therapy (CBT). According to this theory, our thinking has more than one level. This is displayed in the diagram below.

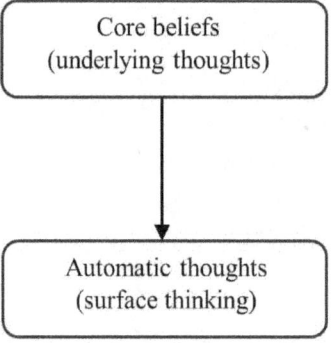

Figure 5: A diagram of the two levels of thought.

Automatic thoughts refer to the running commentary that goes through our heads as we go about our daily lives. If you pay attention, you will notice the constant chatter that goes on in your head about the things you are doing and how you are reacting to the people and events around you.

There is an easy exercise that will show you how this running commentary works. For the next minute, think about a bowl of fruit. Over the course of the minute, just let your thoughts do what they want as you think about a bowl of fruit. At the end of the minute, notice where your thoughts have taken you. Now consider the links between your starting point (thinking about a bowl of fruit) and where you ended up (thinking whatever it was you were thinking). Consider below how this might have played out for one individual. This person started thinking about a bowl of fruit and ended up thinking about a project at work they needed to complete. Follow their automatic thoughts.

> *Ok. I'm thinking about a bowl of fruit. I can picture a bowl of fruit. It's got bananas in it. I like bananas. I should buy some next time I go to the supermarket. I also need to get a loaf of bread. I must start a shopping list. Pay attention and think about a bowl of fruit. Oh, and milk, I mustn't forget milk. I hate running out of milk. Someone said once that they have orange juice on their cereal instead of milk. Yuck. I couldn't imagine anything worse. Not that I eat much cereal. I should eat more cereal... it's probably good for you. I will put cereal on my shopping list. But that might be a waste because I probably won't eat it. I have bought lots of things I thought would be good for me, but I never ate them. That reminds me that I should clean out the pantry. But I won't have the time to do that until I finish the project at work. That will probably take me another week. I have to get feedback from the stakeholders and then finalise my report.*

Core beliefs refer to the underlying beliefs we have about how the world works and how we fit into that world. Core beliefs have influence on our automatic thoughts. That is, we think the things we do on the surface because of our underlying beliefs about how things work. Unlike automatic thoughts, the content of our core beliefs is not readily available to us but can be examined by considering the content of our automatic thoughts.

So, where do the logical errors in thinking we have been talking about fit into this conceptualisation? Let's consider that in the diagram below.

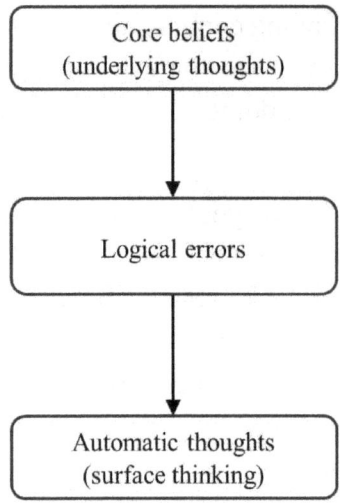

Figure 6: Where errors in thinking occur in our levels of thought.

The errors in thinking we make are a result of the core beliefs we hold. For example, if our core beliefs about the world and the future are that the world is threatening and the outlook is grim and pessimistic, then we are likely to inflate the degree of dangerousness we perceive and we are likely to catastrophise.

These logical errors then affect our surface thinking. We are more likely to be self-critical or tell ourselves everything is hopeless or tell ourselves that nothing is fair because of the logical errors we make based on our particular core beliefs.

Our core beliefs are built on the basis of a variety of influences. These include our genetic makeup (e.g., an inherited overly reactive nervous system), our experiences (the things that happen to us), the messages we receive (the things people have said to us or the way they have treated us), and the ways we have interpreted these events. If the influences are positive and healthy, our core beliefs tend to be clear, and there are few logical errors. If the influences on us are negative, unhealthy or confusing, our core beliefs tend to be inaccurate, and the logical errors we make are many and strongly influence our automatic thoughts.

Underlying assumptions of logical errors

It has been suggested that each logical error is driven by a specific assumption. If our automatic thoughts are biased, then the biases are driven by our core beliefs and assumptions. Below are some examples of cognitive errors and examples of associated assumptions. Here we are referring to the assumptions that are inevitably made if the errors in our thinking are present.

Table 5. The assumptions underlying each logical error.

Cognitive error	Assumption
Filtering	The only events that matter are failures. I should measure myself by my errors.
Polarised thinking	Everything is always one extreme or the other.
Overgeneralisation	If it's true in one case, it must be true in every case that is even slightly similar.
Jumping to conclusions	If it has always been true in the past, it is going to be true in the future.
Catastrophising	Always think the worst because it is most likely to happen to you.
Personalisation	I am responsible for all bad things, failures, etc.
Control fallacies	You should be able to know in advance what is going to happen. You should have seen the bad thing coming before it happened.
Fallacy of fairness	The world is a fair place, and fairness influences how things turn out.
Blaming	Whether it is me or someone else, someone is always responsible when things are not the way I want them to be.
Shoulds	People have an obligation to do specific things that cannot be avoided.
Emotional reasoning	If a person feels bad, something must be wrong.
Fallacy of change	People must change to meet other people's needs.
Global labelling	A whole person and their entire life can be summed up by a single word (e.g., stupid).
Always being right	People have to choose a side, and there is a right side and a wrong side.

| Heaven's reward fallacy | Choosing to do good things for others will oblige others to do good things in return. |

Let's consider how these logical errors and the assumptions that are made affect automatic thoughts. Consider in this example what this person is saying to themselves at a time in their life when they are overwhelmed by the extra demands placed on them.

> *Henry felt he was barely coping. He had a busy job in IT that required him to work long hours. Henry's supervisor left unexpectedly, and Henry agreed to take over that role until the position was filled. This meant that he was doing two jobs when his own position kept him busy and stretched to the limit. When he agreed to take on this additional role, Henry was told that it was only going to be for a short time. However, the weeks turned into months, and no progress was made in filling the position. Henry was struggling to cope. Today, Henry made a mistake that took some time to rectify. This was because he had too much to do, and it was inevitable that he would find it difficult to do everything well. Nevertheless, Henry said the following to himself.*
>
> *"I can't believe I made that mistake. I had to fix the problems it caused, and I apologised to everyone. Everyone was understanding, but I bet they thought I was hopeless and shouldn't be doing the boss' job* (jumping to conclusions). *People aren't going to forget I mucked up... I'm not going to forget. Of all the stupid things to do* (filtering). *And I can't disagree with their view. This mistake just proves I can't be relied on* (overgeneralisation). *Let's face it, I can either do the job properly or I can't* (polarised thinking), *and it turns out I can't."*

Let's break this down and see where this person is making mistakes. This person was obviously overburdened and had made an error as a consequence. It seems that the mistake could be rectified, and it was resolved. Nevertheless, Henry reacted to the mistake poorly and thought in ways that were not helpful.

> To start, Henry jumped to the conclusion that people thought of him as incompetent and that they thought negatively of him. This is despite the fact that the only information he had available to him about the views of others was that they were being understanding.
>
> Henry then went on to focus on the error he made and the perception that judgments about his competence would be based on this one mistake. He failed to take into account the good work he had done over the preceding months, despite being placed under excessive pressure. This is an example of filtering.
>
> Henry then went on to overgeneralise the meaning of the error. He told himself that making one mistake was evidence of his unreliability. This was despite the fact that

he had conducted many tasks over many months while under pressure without making errors of this nature.

Then Henry engaged in 'black-and-white' or polarised thinking. He assumed that there were only two possibilities. That is, he thought that, if an error was made, either he could do the job properly without error or he could not do the job. This type of rigid thinking ignores the fact that people make mistakes all the time, including those who are competent in their jobs. This style of thinking also ignores the fact that he was able to identify the mistake and rectify any problems it might have created.

The errors in Henry's thinking have resulted in him feeling much worse than he would have had his thinking been more balanced. Let's find out how to change these errors in thinking to protect yourself from the negative effects of logical errors.

Understanding automatic thoughts

The goal here is to teach you to think in a more realistic and balanced way so that you can cope better and deal with the fact you have too many stressful things to do. This is done in a number of steps. Let's start this process.

Everybody experiences automatic thoughts. They reflect our way of making sense of and reacting to the world around us and to internal experiences, such as anxiety or memories and urges. Automatic thoughts are often highly believable, even when they are based on logical errors. As a result of their believability, we tend not to challenge them. If they pass unchallenged, they can have a profound and detrimental effect on our emotional state. For example, if a person believes they must please everyone all of the time, they are likely to feel bad if someone expresses displeasure or disagrees with them or in situations where they have to say no to a request being made of them.

Consider this example.

> *This person's goal is always to make sure that people are happy with what she does. She describes herself as a 'people pleaser'. Lately, she has been inundated with extra demands on her time. She feels pushed to her limit. Her elderly parents aren't well. Her father is in hospital and is not doing very well, and her mother is unwell at home. She has had to care for them more than she would normally need to do. She has been dividing her available time between hospital visits and dropping into her mother's home to care for her. She has been busy at work, and she has some outstanding tasks with looming deadlines. Her husband has been stressed about a situation at his work and has wanted to talk in the evenings about how this had made him feel. Also, he will be away from home this weekend because of a work demand that he cannot avoid. Her children have had some additional school and extra-curricular activities that have demanded her time*

> *and attention. This weekend, she has to take them to sporting events and one of them to a friend's birthday party. A friend phones, informing her that she thought she might go away for the weekend with her husband and asks whether she could drop her three children around to stay for the weekend. Let's examine the content of this person's self-talk.*
>
> *"I don't know what to do. I have so much to do, but I don't know how I can handle it all. But I really should help out my friend (shoulds). I don't know how I will cope with her children this weekend. They are a handful at the best of times. But, if I say no, I will be a terrible friend (global labelling). But I really don't know how I will handle all the things I have to do with three extra children and my husband away. I don't know what to do. Really, I should be able to handle what is happening. It is my own fault that I haven't been coping better (blaming). I suppose that if I do the right thing now, it will be my turn to get some help when I need it in the future (Heaven's reward fallacy)."*

It would be hard to think this way without feeling upset with yourself. We tend to believe the things we tell ourselves, even if they are not true. This person is telling herself that she had some sort of requirement to do what was asked of her by a friend despite knowing that it probably was not possible to do all that she had to do this weekend without the support of her husband with the addition of three children as well as her own. Her thoughts were telling her she must agree to her friend's request, making her feel more pressured and desperate than she was already feeling.

Catching automatic thoughts

It is important to pay attention to your automatic thoughts so that their content can be used to identify both the logical errors you are making and, ultimately, your core beliefs. The way to go about this is to keep a thought record related to times when you notice a change in the way you are feeling.

In their simplest form, a thought record asks you to identify the event that has occurred, to take notice of the thoughts that go through your head at the time of the event, and to record the consequences you experience, both in terms of how you feel and how you might act in response. Consider the example below of a simple thought record of a mother of three who has two volunteer positions and who helps her husband in his business without being paid for her work.

A	B	C
Activating event	Belief or thought	Consequence: emotional and behavioural
My brother and sister asked me to select the venue and organise a party for our parents' wedding anniversary because, they said, I throw the best parties.	*My brother and sister always go out of their way to load me up with things to do. I bet it is because they think I have more time than them because I don't have a paid job.*	*I felt so frustrated I rang them both and told them they were only doing this because they hated me.*
My family disagreed with my decision to have a theme for the party.	*They are just wrong about this. I'm not giving in on this. I will show them.*	*I felt really angry. I went ahead and ordered invitations with the theme I chose.*

We do not usually pay much deliberate attention to the fact that we are having thoughts going through our heads, even though they can have such a profound effect on how we are feeling and what we choose to do as a result of feeling that way. To change our thinking, we have to learn to identify our automatic thoughts. When we consider the events that trigger a response in us, we can usually identify what went through our mind at the time.

By keeping track of your automatic thoughts, you can learn about patterns in your thinking that are linked with particular negative feelings and the behaviours you choose because you are feeling that way. Use the simple thought record below to keep track of your automatic thoughts in relation to events that stress you.

Simple automatic thoughts worksheet		
A	B	C
Activating event	Belief or thought	Consequence: emotional and behavioural

Worksheet available at elemen.com.au

Understanding and noticing logical errors

Everyone makes logical errors. It is important to understand this point. It is when the error you are making (e.g., everything should be fair) conflicts with how things really are (e.g., the world is neither fair nor unfair, it just is the way it is) that problems arise. It is also important to be able to recognise the logical errors you are making so that you can correct them and correct the problems in your core beliefs. To start to do this, you can try the simple approach of expanding on your thought record form so that you include the types of logical errors that are reflected in your automatic thoughts.

Let's go back to our original thought record form and expand the examples.

Expanded thought record form - example			
A	B	C	D
Activating event	Belief or thought	Consequence: emotional and behavioural	Logical errors
My brother and sister asked me to select the venue and organise a party for our parents' wedding anniversary because, they said, I throw the best parties.	*My brother and sister always go out of their way to load me up with things to do. I bet it is because they think I have more time than them because I don't have a paid job.*	*I felt so frustrated I rang them both and told them they were only doing this because they hated me.*	*Jumping to conclusions*
My family disagreed with my decision to have a theme for the party.	*They are just wrong about this. I'm not giving in on this. I will show them.*	*I felt really angry. I went ahead and ordered invitations with the theme I chose.*	*Always being right*

Despite this person's brother and sister giving a reason for making the request, that is, their sibling is a good party organiser, this person has jumped to the conclusions that they have a different reason for their request. In this way, this person has reached a conclusion that is unwarranted and without evidence. This has caused them to feel frustrated. They then felt driven to escalate the problem by phoning the siblings to express their unhappiness.

Against the views of all other family members, this person chose a theme for the party. This person was determined to show they were right despite this decision causing more work for them. The anger felt in response to the rejection of the theme idea triggered a determination to prove the rightness of the idea by going ahead and ordering the invitations that, in effect, forced the issue.

Below is an expanded thought record form that you can use to identify your logical errors in what you are thinking.

Expanded thought record form			
A	B	C	D
Activating event	Belief or thought	Consequence: emotional and behavioural	Logical errors

Worksheet available at elemen.com.au

Reframing your thoughts (cognitive restructuring)

The process of challenging our negative automatic thoughts is called cognitive restructuring. This is what we are trying to achieve here. The conclusions we reach because of our logical errors should be challenged and replaced with something that is healthier and more accurately reflects how the world really works.

Although there are lots of ways you can go about restructuring your thinking, we are going to introduce you to a straightforward method. We are going to start by ensuring that you understand the difference between fact and opinion. This is important as our thoughts and decision-making should be based on facts and not the opinions we form because of incorrect information that can underlie our core beliefs. For example, an opinion would be "I am stupid". You might form this opinion because someone has repeatedly told you that you are stupid or because they acted in a way that encouraged you to believe you are stupid. It is not the truth or a fact that you are stupid even if you sometimes to unwise things. It is a belief you have or an opinion you have formed because of incorrect information.

We refer to the opinion on which you rely as a work of fiction. That is, you write a story in your head about what is happening and then act as if the story is true. You need to be able to identify when you are relying on the story you have written in your mind rather than basing your thoughts on factual evidence. Let's start by having a go at identifying fact from opinion or fiction. In the spaces provided, you can add other things you have been thinking and consider whether they are facts or opinions.

Fact or fiction worksheet		
Statement	*Fact*	*Fiction*
I am stupid		√
I love bushwalking	√	
I am ugly		
I forgot to renew my driver's licence		
No one likes me		
This will be a disaster		
I'm not good enough		
I should be able to control things		
I hate my job		
There are times when people feel stressed		

Checklist available at elemen.com.au

The facts here are:

> I love bushwalking
>
> I forgot to renew my driver's licence
>
> I hate my job
>
> There are times when people feel stressed

The statements that are opinions are:

> I am stupid
>
> I am ugly
>
> No one likes me
>
> This will be a disaster
>
> I'm not good enough
>
> I should be able to control things

Why should we make this distinction between what is a fact and what is an opinion? It is because the errors in thinking we make are based on opinion and not on fact. Further, because we hold this opinion, we assume that it is true because we are thinking it and not because it is based on fact.

To tidy up our thinking and remove the logical errors, we have to rely on those thoughts that are based on fact alone. We can reject thoughts that are just based on our opinions because our opinions can be faulty. Factual information will be a good guide for us to determine whether or not we should believe what we are thinking.

Cognitive restructuring worksheet – Example
What I am thinking *My brother and sister always go out of their way to load me up with things to do. They think I have more time because I don't have a paid job.*
Facts supporting the thought *They asked me to organise the party.*
Facts contradicting the thought *They said I organise the best parties.* *I have organised good parties in the past.* *My siblings have commented before on how impressed they have been with the parties I have thrown.* *My brother and sister have told me that I work too hard and take on too much.*
Is this thought based on factual evidence or opinion? *This thought was just based on my opinion. I just thought they were picking on me because I am not working. They never said any such thing.*

By looking at the facts for and against a point of view being true, you can work out the value of holding that opinion. It seems like a waste of time to be thinking a particular thing and being negatively affected by it emotionally and behaviourally if you cannot even determine that the opinion reflects the truth. You can use the worksheet below to examine your thoughts in terms of the facts supporting what you are thinking and the facts that contradict what you are thinking.

Cognitive restructuring worksheet
What I am thinking
Facts supporting the thought
Facts contradicting the thought
Is this thought based on factual evidence or opinion?

Worksheet available at elemen.com.au

Making the restructured thinking habitual

To get to a point where you are thinking in a healthier way, you need to go through a process of deliberately challenging your thinking. You need to overlearn to notice your automatic thoughts and then reframe them into a healthier and more accurate alternative thought. You will then challenge your thinking and adjust your automatic thoughts without giving it much attention. Eventually, you will not even have to do that because your core beliefs will be corrected to offer you a more accurate template of how the world works and how you fit into that world.

Targeting the assumptions

Let's not forget about those assumptions that underlie the errors you make in your thinking. You need to challenge those assumptions to completely correct your thinking. Remember, if the assumptions that underlie the error are shown to be wrong, there is every reason to abandon the logical error and replace it with a more logical point of view.

There are a few ways you can challenge the assumptions that underlie logical errors. We are going to focus on three approaches. Firstly, we are going to apply the strategy of looking at the advantages and disadvantages of holding an assumption. Consider the following example of someone who always has to be right.

Logical error and assumption
Always being right. People have to choose a side, and there is a right side and a wrong side.
Advantages
It is satisfying to be proven right.
Disadvantages
I will be facing a lot of conflict with people if I continue to assume I am always right. *I will be disappointed throughout life if I am not more flexible in my thinking.* *There are lots of situations in life where there is no right and wrong side and I am going to have a difficult life if I don't accept this.*

Challenging the assumption that underlies a tendency to want to always be right, you can see that there are many more disadvantages to doing this than there are advantages. The disadvantages indicate that the holder of the assumption is facing ongoing difficulties if they continue to hold this point of view.

Secondly, you can act against the assumptions. What would happen if the assumption was incorrect? Consider the following example.

Logical error and assumption
Always being right. People have to choose a side, and there is a right side and a wrong side.

Things that might happen if I acted like the assumption was not true
I might relax instead of fighting for my point of view all the time.
I might find that I have fewer conflicts with people.
I might feel less of a burden of responsibility to be in charge of everything.

By acting as if the assumption is false, you can usually identify the positive things that would occur as a consequence. All of these things are better than fighting to be right about everything. Remember, trying always to be right is stressful and exhausting.

Finally, you can argue against the assumption. You can take the perspective that the assumption is wrong and develop an argument for your case. Consider the following example.

Logical error and assumption
Always being right. People have to choose a side, and there is a right side and a wrong side.

Arguments against the assumption
It is not possible to always be right about everything.
People are entitled to their own opinions.
There are lots of things in life that are a matter of point of view, so they are not a matter of right or wrong.

Here, you are thinking of the *facts* that can be used to present a good argument that the assumption associated with the logical error is not accurate. This will allow you to challenge your error-ridden thinking and replace it with healthier thinking that will not encourage you to feel strong, negative emotions. Can you think of other arguments you could use against the assumption?

Below is a worksheet you can use to challenge the assumptions that underlie your errors in thinking.

Targeting assumptions worksheet
Logical error and assumption
Advantages
Disadvantages
Things that might happen if I acted like the assumption was not true
Arguments against the assumption

Worksheet is available at elemen.com.au

Here, we have asked you to consider challenging the sorts of thoughts you might have that are likely to make you feel worse than you would otherwise feel if you did not think that way. You have learned to access these logical errors by paying attention to your automatic thoughts that serve as the running commentary your mind provides. You have learned ways to challenge these errors and remove them and their influence from your thinking. The goal of doing these things has been to help you manage your distress and protect yourself from distress in the future.

Improving your coping skills

We are going to examine ways you cope and how you can use those ways of coping. We will explore the fact that people have preferred styles of coping, and your best chance of coping well is to build up your coping strategies in the way that best suits you. Let's start to explore coping in general and your preferred coping style.

Coping

We all have our own coping resources and individual coping skills. This is because there is not one particular way of coping. In a general sense, the way you will cope with having too many stressful things to do will likely be a reflection of the way you have dealt with and solved other problems throughout your life. That is, the way you cope will reflect your general style of coping.

Your goal should be to understand how you cope and to make good use of the coping resources you have or can create, as well as the particular skills you have developed or can develop. This is true even if you take into account the fact that dealing with your current stressful overload may be a more challenging problem than other problems you have dealt with in your life. For those of you who feel you do not cope well with life problems, it may be the case you have been trying to develop coping skills based on a pattern of coping that does not suit you.

To understand the way you cope and to use this knowledge to choose the best strategies to cope with having too many stressful things happening at once, consideration needs to be given to the fundamental differences people can have in the way they approach problem situations. Let's consider the different approaches to coping so that you can work out your own preferred coping style.

Problem-focused coping vs. emotion-focused coping

To start, a distinction can be made between problem-focused coping strategies and emotion-focused strategies.

Who are problem-focused copers?

Problem-focused copers deal with their problems by considering the problem situation and trying to fix it. They tend to want to *do* something when they are confronted with a problem. They are most comfortable when there are specific things related to the problem that can be the focus of their attention. In the context of having too many stressful things to do, a problem-focused coper might write down a plan for completing all the important tasks they need to get done.

Who are emotion-focused copers?

Emotion-focused copers are the people who deal with their problems by expressing their emotional reactions to the situation. They will talk about the problem and cry when they feel the need. They see the value of looking to others to share their feelings about their problem. In the context of having too many stressful things to do, an emotion-focused coper might have a good cry to let go of some of the stress before moving on to undertake the tasks they are facing.

Are people either emotion-focused or problem-focused copers?

Some people are strongly problem-focused copers and some people are strongly emotion-focused copers. Others fall somewhere on the continuum between the two extreme positions. You may be more problem-focused than emotion-focused but still make use of some emotion-focused strategies… or the reverse.

You will be able to do a little exercise to find your coping preferences or to confirm them if you already have a good idea of where on the continuum you fall. But, first, we have to consider one other element.

Problem-approach vs. problem-avoidance copers

People assume that when we talk about coping strategies, we are referring to good ones that will help us deal with the problems we face. This is not the case. People's coping style can be divided on the basis of whether they tend to front up to their problems or whether they prefer to avoid them. This is the case for both problem-focused copers and emotion-focused copers.

Let's start by looking at problem-focused coping. How would problem approach and problem avoidance strategies differ? Consider the examples in the table below.

Table 6: Examples of problem-focused approach and avoidance strategies.

Problem-focused approach strategies	Problem-focused avoidance strategies
Problem solving Problem solving coping strategies involve: Examining the problem Generating potential solutions Evaluating the likelihood of a successful outcome Moving forward and applying the strategy	*Problem avoidance* Problem avoidance coping strategies involve: Deliberately avoiding thinking about the problem Deliberately avoiding reminders of the problem
Cognitive restructuring Cognitive restructuring coping strategies involve: Reframing your thoughts to think more reasonably about the problem Correcting errors in thinking that are barriers to coping with the problem	*Wishful thinking* Wishful thinking as a coping strategy involves: Wishing the problem would go away Indulging in thoughts that things will return to 'normal' Spending time thinking about how things will work out in your favour and as you wish

With regard to having too many stressful things happening at once, effective problem-focused approach coping strategies may help in the following ways. They may help you generate ideas of how to solve specific problems you face, such as accepting some help. They may also help you to work out ways that you can cope more effectively with the demands being placed on you, such as deciding that it is acceptable to take some time out for yourself even if you have lots to do.

Now, let's consider emotion-focused coping. The table below details examples of approach and avoidance emotion-focused coping strategies.

Table 7: Examples of emotion-focused approach and avoidance strategies.

Emotion-focused approach strategies	Emotion-focused avoidance strategies
Emotion expression Emotion expression as a coping strategy involves: Being open and talking about how you are feeling Allowing yourself to experience your emotional reactions in relation to the problem Using emotional expression as a form of catharsis, letting off steam to allow yourself to feel better for a while	*Self-criticism* Self-criticism as a coping strategy involves: Blaming yourself for the problem Criticising yourself for failing to control your emotional reaction to the problem Viewing yourself as more generally deficient than is warranted
Social support Using social support as a coping strategy involves: Turning to family and friends for support Talking with your support network about how you are feeling Taking comfort from your support people Allowing your support network to offer instrumental support*	*Social withdrawal* Social withdrawal as a copy strategy involves: Cutting yourself off from family and friends Failing to seek professional support when it is needed Refusing assistance offered by the people who wish to help you or would be willing to do so

* Instrumental support refers to things others might do to help you, such as collect your children from school or cook some meals for you.

When we consider having too many stressful things to do, the effective emotion-focused approach coping strategies may be of assistance to you in the following ways.

They may allow you to express your emotional reactions and deal with them rather than bottle them up. They may result in you choosing to seek support from your family and friends to allow you to discuss how you are feeling and, potentially, resolve some of those feelings that can be overwhelming if they are kept hidden.

Identifying your preferred coping style

The goal here is to identify the type of coping that works best for you. If you are an emotion-focused coper, you may see the value of a problem-focused coping approach, but it is unlikely that you could comfortably adopt problem-focused coping strategies and expect them to work for you. Your efforts would be better directed at taking advantage of your preferred style of coping and using problem-approach strategies.

Here is an exercise to determine what type of coping style best characterises your preferred type. Tick the boxes if you typically use the listed coping strategy.

	How do I normally cope?
Problem solving	
☐	I work on finding ways to solve the problems I face.
☐	I work out what I should do, and then I follow the plan.
☐	I like to work out a plan and then move forward.
☐	I believe there is a solution to every problem.
Problem avoidance	
☐	I try to act like nothing is wrong.
☐	When faced with a problem, I choose not to do anything, even when I know I should.
☐	I try not to spend any time thinking about the problem.
☐	When the problem comes to mind, I push it out of my head.
Cognitive restructuring	
☐	I think about my problems in a way that allows me to realise I can manage them.
☐	I think about the problem to change the way I react to it.
☐	I try to look on the bright side of any situation.
☐	I try to put things into perspective.

Wishful thinking	
	When faced with a problem, I just wish it would go away.
	I just hope a miracle will happen to make everything all right.
	I hope the problem will fix itself.
	I wish that someone would come and fix the problem for me.
Emotion expression	
	When faced with a problem, I allow myself to express my feelings about it.
	I do not try to bottle up my feelings; I let them go so that I can feel better.
	I do not hide my feelings about the problem from other people.
	When faced with a problem, I just need some time to experience my feelings.
Self-criticism	
	I blame myself for the problem I am facing.
	I ask myself what I have done to make the problem happen.
	I tend to hold myself responsible for the problems I face.
	When a problem occurs, I feel I should have done things differently.
Social support	
	I turn to the people I know will listen when I talk about how I feel.
	I feel better when I can talk to others about my problems.
	When faced with a problem, I seek advice from people I trust.
	I allow other people to offer help and support when I am dealing with a problem.

	Social withdrawal
	When faced with a problem, I like to avoid other people and spend time by myself.
	When I am struggling with a problem, I do not want to be around other people.
	I do not share my thoughts and feelings with others.
	I do not accept the help others offer.

Checklist available at elemen.com.au

What type of coper are you? Add up the ticks you have placed in each of the categories and enter the number in the following table.

Ways of coping score sheet	
Problem-focused strategies	*Emotion-focused strategies*
_____ Problem-solving _____ Cognitive restructuring _____ Problem avoidance _____ Wishful thinking _____ Total	_____ Emotion expression _____ Social support _____ Self-criticism _____ Social withdrawal _____ Total
Problem-approach strategies	*Problem-avoidance strategies*
_____ Problem-solving _____ Cognitive restructuring _____ Emotion expression _____ Social support _____ Total	_____ Problem-avoidance _____ Wishful thinking _____ Self-criticism _____ Social withdrawal _____ Total

Score sheet available at elemen.com.au

When comparing your problem-focused and emotion-focused strategies, see where you have scored the highest. This may show a strong preference for one type of coping strategy or the other. If so, you can build on your preferred coping type when you consider what coping strategies will help you with your current situation. If you have similar totals for both problem-focused and emotion-focused strategies, you would do best to include each type in your coping plan.

When considering whether you use problem-approach strategies or problem-avoidance strategies, you are considering whether adjustments have to be made in the way you cope. If you predominantly use problem-avoidance strategies, you can learn to abandon those in favour of problem-approach strategies while staying within the same style of coping strategy, that is, problem-focused or emotion-focused.

Building your coping repertoire

Now that you better understand the ways you cope, you can start to build a plan of how you are going to move forward, adopting coping strategies that work for you. Let's consider some examples of coping strategies you could adopt.

Problem-focused strategies

We will start by looking at problem-solving strategies. Here you are trying to work out a plan of how you would go about solving a specific problem situation, followed by decision-making with regard to which potential solution you would choose. You then should be able to follow through and solve your problem.

Let's consider an example of this process.

Example of a problem-solving strategy
What is the problem? Clearly define the problem you are facing.
The problem I am facing is that I have too many things to do and not enough time to do them all. I have become overwhelmed by all the demands that have been placed on me.

Generate as many possible solutions as you can. List the ones that are likely to work.

I could do the following:

> *I could just keep doing what I have been doing and hope I can find the time to do everything.*
>
> *I could ask my boss for some extra help and look at the possibility of getting some help at home.*
>
> *I could learn to manage my time better and prioritise things that are important.*

Consider the likelihood of each of these strategies being successful.

If I keep doing things the way I have been doing them, it doesn't seem likely that this would work. I am already exhausted, and I just don't see how I can keep up the pace for an extended period of time. It doesn't seem likely that I could do this without burning out and becoming unwell myself.

I could investigate what assistance is available at work and with home help. If I could get some home help and this person did some of the housework, for example, this would free me up to do some of the other things on my list of things to do. With the help of someone else, the number of things I have to do would lessen. If I got some help at work, my excessive workload would lighten.

I could learn to manage my time better. The trouble with this idea is that learning time management skills would probably just free me up to take on more jobs. If I was able to get more time, I would prefer to use that time to do some things that are enjoyable, such as some leisure time for me. I might be able to generate some more time but the number of jobs I have to do wouldn't reduce.

Select the problem-solving strategy that is likely to work the best.

I choose to explore getting some help at work and some home help. This is the option that would both reduce the number of things I have to do and give me more time to do some things for myself which I need.

What are you going to do next?

I am going to talk to my boss about some assistance and I am going to explore what cleaning services are available to me for help at home.

In this example, the person has thought about the problem and identified possible options for resolving it. The person then considered what the likely outcome for each possible solution would be. They then chose their preferred solution and worked out a plan for their next step. This is a good problem-solving approach.

Below is a worksheet you can use to develop problem-solving coping strategies.

A problem-solving strategy worksheet
What is the problem? Clearly define the problem you are facing.
Generate as many possible solutions as you can. List the ones that are likely to work.
Consider the likelihood of each of these strategies being successful.
Select the problem-solving strategy that is likely to work the best.
What are you going to do next?

Worksheet available at elemen.com.au

Now, let's consider a cognitive restructuring approach to coping. Remember, cognitive restructuring refers to changing the way you think about a problem. Below is an example of a cognitive restructuring approach to addressing a problem situation.

Example of a cognitive restructuring strategy
What is the problem? *I have so much to do that I am not able to do things to the standard I would normally expect of myself.*
What are you thinking? *I think I am not doing a good enough job. People might think I am not doing a good enough job.*
What evidence do you have that this is true? *I usually set high standards, but I have not been able to achieve this.*
What evidence do you have against this being true? *Things are getting done. My family and friends and my boss actually tell me I am doing a good job.*
Even if it was true, what is the worst thing that would happen? *Well, nothing really. I only have to please myself and my boss and my boss understands I am overloaded.*
What do you conclude? *I am probably doing a good enough job, given the difficult circumstances I am facing. My work is getting done, and that is the most important thing. It doesn't really matter what other people think because they are not in my position.*

Here, the person in this example challenged the way they were thinking about their situation. They examined whether the situation was as bad as they were interpreting it to be. Having realised that was not the case, they then worked out a better and more realistic way of thinking about their problem. You can see that their alternative thoughts about their situation would make it easier for them to cope. They would not be tormented by thoughts that they were not good enough. Instead, they could be more accepting of their situation and realise that it is not something they really have to worry about.

Below is a worksheet you can use for cognitive restructuring coping strategies.

A cognitive restructuring strategy worksheet
What is the problem?
What are you thinking?
What evidence do you have that this is true?
What evidence do you have against this being true?
Even if it was true, what is the worst thing that would happen?
What do you conclude?

Worksheet available at elemen.com.au

Next, we will consider how to enhance your emotion expression coping skills.

Example of an emotion expression strategy
What is the problem? *I got more bad news from my boss. She told me my colleague would not be returning for another month at least and I was being asked to continue covering her job while also doing mine for that time.*
What did you do? *I tried to pretend that everything was all right. I pretended to be ok with this news and just went back to my desk.*
What were the advantages of doing this? *I don't really know. I just felt like I was pretending… I was pretending. My boss might have been relieved but I was facing another month of being pushed beyond my limits.*
What were the disadvantages of doing this? *I felt like my head was going to explode. I felt like I was going to fall apart. I worried that if I fell apart there would be no one to do my job or my colleague's job and everyone would be let down. Also, by not saying anything, my boss wasn't aware that I am stressed.*
What could you have done differently? *I could have expressed how I was really feeling about the news. I could have told my boss I needed some of the extra work shared around.*
What would the advantages have been of doing things this other way? *I would have felt some relief. I wouldn't have felt like my head was about to explode and I would have got rid of the knot I feel in my stomach. If I had dealt with my emotions I would have made it clear how this was affecting me and I might have got some help as a result.*
Would there have been any disadvantage of doing things this other way? *Not that I can think of.*
What will you do next time you feel like this? *Next time I will be honest about my emotions and express them in a way that lets me manage the news better and ask for help.*

In this case, the person went through a process of examining the pros and cons of both not expressing their emotions and expressing their emotions in response to the news they received. The conclusion was reached that the better option was to allow themselves to react in a genuine way to what they were feeling.

Below is a worksheet you can use to work on emotion expression coping strategies.

An emotion expression strategy worksheet
What is the problem?
What did you do?
What were the advantages of doing this?
What were the disadvantages of doing this?
What could you have done differently?
What would the advantages have been of doing things this other way?
Would there have been any disadvantage of doing things this other way?

What will you do next time you feel like this?

Worksheet available at elemen.com.au

Finally, we can consider how to use social support as a coping strategy.

Example of social support as a strategy
What is the problem? *In the lead up to the deadline for the completion of the project at work, I have had to work extra hours. To make things worse, my husband is away on a business trip. The problem is that I can't get away to pick up the children from school and spend time with them. They have had to go to afterschool care. Then I pick up something for them to eat on the way home so they are not eating as well as they would normally.*
What have you done in response to this problem? *I have worried about neglecting the children's needs.*
How has responding in this way helped you with your problem? *It hasn't helped. It makes it harder to concentrate on the work I have to do, so it is taking longer, and I have to work longer hours to compensate.*
What could you do instead? *I could ask my mother and my sister to look after the children after school while I am so busy at work and, perhaps, to prepare some meals for me.*
How would this be likely to work out? *The children love spending time with their grandmother and their aunt. If they both helped, it wouldn't be too much of a burden on each of them... not that they would see it as a burden. Also, they both love to cook and would be happy to prepare some meals for us.*
So, what are you going to do next? *I am going to call them both straight away and ask if they will help me.*

Here, the person has thought through their situation and realised that by trying to do everything herself, she was just making things more difficult. She realised a solution was available to her so she reached out to the people who would be happy to support her with the intention of asking them to help. It was an easy thing for her to do and would result in a better situation for her children and herself.

Below is a worksheet you can use for social support coping strategies.

Social support strategy worksheet
What is the problem?
What have you done in response to this problem?
How has responding in this way helped you with your problem?
What could you do instead?
How would this be likely to work out?
So, what are you going to do next?

Worksheet available at elemen.com.au

In moving forward, remember to choose the coping strategy that best suits your preferred coping style. Always choose approach strategies rather than avoidance strategies, no matter what your coping style.

Understand your rights

We are often not clear about our rights, particularly those that relate to our ability to take charge of our lives. Let's look at some of the mistaken assumptions we make that may be related to your current situation and your legitimate rights. We will also consider how holding these mistaken assumptions might affect how you deal with having too many stressful things to do and how abandoning the mistaken assumption may improve your situation.

Table 8: Mistaken assumptions, their consequences and your legitimate rights.

Mistaken assumption	*It is selfish to put your needs before the needs of others.*
Consequence	You may end up not receiving the help and support you need to deal with the stress in your own life. This is because you may not ask for help and support for yourself if you think others are too busy with their own lives.
Legitimate right	You have a right to put yourself first some of the time.
Outcome	Understanding your rights may allow you to ask for the help and support you need at this difficult time. The extent to which a person can offer you help and support should be determined by them and not by you.
Mistaken assumption	*You shouldn't take up other's valuable time with your own problems.*
Consequence	No one knows you need help because you didn't say so. As a consequence, you don't receive the help you need.
Legitimate right	You have a right to ask for help or emotional support.
Outcome	The people who care about you will understand you need help, and they can offer you help if they are able.
Mistaken assumption	*People don't want to hear that you feel bad, so keep it to yourself.*
Consequence	Your feelings are never expressed, and you end up feeling bottled up and isolated.

Legitimate right	You have a right to feel and express how stressed you feel.
Outcome	You will be able to feel some relief by sharing how you feel. Your emotional pain is not harmful to others who care about you. Friendships should be equal and reciprocal in that you should support your friends, and they should support you at times of stress. Accepting that people may be concerned about you frees you to express how you are feeling and allows your friends to do something for you at a time when it probably seems to them there is little they can do to make things better.
Mistaken assumption	*When someone takes the time to give you advice, you should take it seriously.*
Consequence	You may be overwhelmed by people who are telling you what you should do. Unfortunately, the advice from one person can conflict with the advice from another which only increases your confusion.
Legitimate right	You have a right to ignore the advice of others.
Outcome	You will come to realise that the advice people give you is only their opinion and the final decision will be yours to make. You would not then feel pressured to do what others demand or expect, even if it contradicts with what you need
Mistaken assumption	*You should always try to accommodate others. If you don't, they won't be there when you need them.*
Consequence	You will be so busy thinking about what others need that you will have no opportunity to consider your own needs.
Legitimate right	You have a right to say no.
Outcome	You are the only person who truly knows how you are feeling so you need to be the person who decides what you can take on and what you cannot. By understanding you have the right to say no, you can pay attention to your own needs when they are greater than the needs of others.

Mistaken assumption	*Don't be anti-social. People are going to think you don't like them if you say you'd rather be alone instead of with them.*
Consequence	You will have no opportunity to have time by yourself to compensate for how busy you have been and how you are feeling if you give in to the demands of others to do what they are offering.
Legitimate right	You have a right to be alone, even if others would prefer your company.
Outcome	By understanding you have a right to time to yourself, you may be able to strike a good balance between being around others and being alone to balance the pressures in your life.
Mistaken assumption	*You should have a good reason for what you feel and do.*
Consequence	You waste energy thinking about how you are presenting yourself to others and worrying about what they think about you.
Legitimate right	You have a right not to have to justify yourself to others.
Outcome	Particularly at times of intense stress, you should be able to express yourself without having to explain yourself to others who may have chosen to do things differently if they were in your situation.
Mistaken assumption	*When someone is in trouble, you should help them.*
Consequence	This may cause you to ignore your own needs in favour of the needs of others. This can result in your needs never being met and you feel even more overloaded.
Legitimate right	You have a right not to take responsibility for someone else's problem.
Outcome	There are times in life when your needs exceed the needs of others, even if they are facing problems of their own. Understanding this may free you to focus on your own emotional reactions without worrying about the emotional reactions of others.

Mistaken assumption	*It is not nice to put people off. If questioned, give an answer.*
Consequence	Believing this, you may feel pressured to discuss things you do not want to discuss at times when you are not feeling able to discuss them or find yourself agreeing to things you might not agree to if you had more time to consider.
Legitimate right	You have a right to choose not to respond to a situation.
Outcome	Pressure on the part of the questioner does not give them the right to know or you an obligation to respond to their questioning. You are the person who decides when you respond. By accepting this, you can maintain some control over how you respond and in what timeframe you respond.

In many cases, asserting your legitimate rights is largely a matter of you accepting that these rights are legitimate and then calmly acting on that understanding. However, you may also wish to be prepared to assertively express your needs and negotiate for an outcome that works for you.

Assertive negotiation

When learning to manage the stressors in your life, it is not the goal to just put your head down and accept your difficult situation. It is important that you learn to negotiate for what you want without disregarding what the other person might want. What we are referring to here is assertive negotiation.

Assertiveness refers to standing up for your rights without trampling over the rights of others. Some people mistake assertiveness for aggressiveness, which refers to the aggressive assertion of your rights irrespective of others' rights. The other extreme is passivity, where a person will not stand up for their own rights and allow others to walk over them.

So, the aim here is to teach you to stand up for your own rights without trampling over the rights of other people. An assertive interpersonal style will allow you to negotiate for what you want without demanding that it happen.

Asking for change

Firstly, we need to consider how to assertively solve problems by making reasonable requests for change or appropriate requests for what you would like to have happen. Many people find this difficult. They will start to make a request but are easily derailed by the deflection techniques used by the other person. Alternatively, they will start to make a request but are then affected by the annoyance they feel about the response of the other person. The following step-by-step guide is designed to help you plan ahead for how you are going to manage a request for change.

Define the problem situation

You should start by defining the problem you are facing. Do this by focusing on the facts of the matter and not your interpretation of the situation. You should do this by being as specific as possible. Avoid generalisations like "It's always the case…" or "Nothing ever goes right…". So, keep a narrow focus on the situation you have identified that you wish to change. Limit this to one problem at a time rather than bombarding the other person with a list of grievances.

> *My problem is that my work tasks are coming from three senior staff, all of whom insist that their work should take priority.*

Describe how you are feeling

Here, you get a chance to describe how you feel about the situation. Remember, you are referring to how you feel and not how someone else *made* you feel. Be clear about the link between your feelings and the problem situation. Again, do not generalise to all situations or all problems.

Avoid blaming others. By blaming others, you put them on the defensive and little is ever resolved as a consequence. When you talk about how you are feeling, use what is called an 'I message'. That is, your descriptions of your feelings should start with something like "I feel…". No one can argue with you about this matter. They cannot say that you do not feel something that you have stated you feel. If you started with "You make me feel…", it is likely the other person would argue that it was not their intention to make you feel that way, and if you do, that is your problem. Using 'I messages' allows you to avoid all of this discussion. In any case, you are the person who decides how you feel, and you should be able to relate that feeling to the other person.

This is a good opportunity to express your feelings. It is a mistake to assume that others know what you are thinking or feeling if you have not said so. If you have not said how you feel, the other person can do little more than guess. We make a mistake by assuming that someone who knows you well can 'mindread' and automatically know what you are thinking or feeling. Clear communication works much better than allowing others to guess.

> *I feel anxious about these competing demands. I also feel resentful that my concerns about this are dismissed or ignored.*

Make your request for change

Here, you should make a statement about what you want to happen. You need to be brief. Do not turn your request into a lecture. Also, you need to be specific. Clearly state what you want rather than use terms that are not concrete. For example, it will not help to say, "I want things to improve" because that is a generalised statement that can be interpreted in a multitude of ways. You would be better off saying, "I want you to cook dinner two nights a week," or "I am asking you to change your work hours so that you start an hour earlier and finish an hour earlier".

> *I want you, as my manager, to fix this situation by taking on the responsibility of prioritising the tasks and informing others that this is what is occurring.*

Outline possible positive consequences

If the other person initially does not want to agree with your request for change, you may choose to point out the positive consequences that would follow from the agreement. Do not make wild promises. Just focus on the positive things that are likely to happen from the change you are requesting. You are building the argument for what you want. For example, you could say, "I am asking you to change your work hours so that you start an hour earlier and finish an hour earlier. If you agree, you will be able to leave before the peak hour traffic and have more time in the evenings".

> *If you agree, I will be able to make better progress in completing the tasks because my time will not be taken up with dealing with the demands for priority. My performance will also improve if my anxiety is resolved.*

Outline potential negative consequences

If the other person is still reluctant to agree with what you are asking, you can outline the likely negative consequences for them if they choose not to comply with your wishes. Do not threaten. Simply state what you understand to be the bad things that will happen if things do not change. For example, you could say, "I am asking you to change your work hours so that you start an hour earlier and finish an hour earlier. If you disagree, I will have to employ someone to start early. As I cannot just employ them for an hour, I will have to cut back your hours in the mornings so I can get someone to start at the earlier time".

It is important to remember that you should only outline negative consequences that you are certain you are willing to follow through on. You, too, have to live with the negative consequences, so do not outline something you are not willing to do or to have happen.

> *If you feel this is something you are not prepared to do, I will have to contact HR to discuss the pressure of the unreasonable demands I am facing every day. I will do this in an effort to resolve my problem.*

So, to summarise, when making a request for change, do the following:

- Define the problem situation
- Describe how you are feeling
- Make your request for change
- Outline possible positive consequences
- Outline potential negative consequences

This is a good approach to standing up for your rights in an assertive manner. It is relatively simple and straightforward. You can also work out in advance what it is you want to say and this protects you from having to make it up on the spot.

However, standing up for your rights may not be enough in itself if you are aiming for assertive communication. You need to be able to negotiate for what you want with a person who may be inclined not to give this to you. Consider the following negotiation process.

Negotiating for what you want

To negotiate with another person, your starting point needs to be that you both have needs that are equally important. This will require some effort on your part. It is easy for us to assume that what we want is right and what the other person wants is wrong. However, if you hold this view, then any interaction about the issue in question will be an argument rather than a negotiation.

There are six steps that should be taken when you enter into a negotiation. Let's consider each of these steps.

Know what it is you want

Know what it is that you are negotiating for. You must have a clearly defined goal if you are to enter into a negotiation. If you are not clear about what you want then how can the other person have any idea?

Make a statement of what you want in specific terms

In specific terms and being as clear as possible, make a statement about what you want or do not want to have happen. This can be in terms of what you want or do not want the other person to do. However, it may also be in terms of what you want as the outcome.

Listen to the point of view of the other person

Your goal here is to understand the other person's perspective. To do this, you have to listen carefully to what the other person has to say about their point of view. You should use active listening skills where you can ask for clarification or elaboration. Remember, you may not agree with the other person's perspective. What you should be doing is appreciating that they have a point of view that might be different from yours, but it is their point of view nonetheless.

Make a proposal

Next, you should make a proposal that offers a resolution. The proposal should not be solely based on what you want. It should take into account the other person's needs. This can be a challenging step that may take some thought on your part. It is easier to conceptualise a proposal that takes into account what both of you want if you approach it with the goal of achieving a 'win-win' outcome. This is where you get some of what you want, and the other person gets some of what they want. A win-win proposal has a much better chance of being accepted than a 'my way or the highway' approach.

Ask for a counterproposal

If your proposal is not accepted, do not be disheartened. Ask the other person for a counterproposal. Remember that your goal is to reach a point where you can both accept the proposal, even if you both do not get all of what you want.

Aim for compromise

The end result of any negotiation is typically a compromise. You are unlikely to get everything your way, but neither is the other person. You are aiming to reach a middle point that is satisfactory to you both. There are a variety of ways a compromise can be achieved:

> You give up some of what you want to gain some of what you want, and so does the other person.

> You might split the difference.

> You might agree that you do it your way when you are in control, and the other person does it their way when they are in control.

Remember, the goal here is to negotiate for what you want rather than demand. A negotiated agreement may call for compromise but should be positive for both you and the other person in some ways.

Achieving some balance

It is important that you have the opportunity to do some things for yourself. Having a balance between the tasks that are important that you must undertake and some leisure time will improve the balance of your life.

With limited time available to you, it is important that you choose activities that are meaningful to you and will improve the satisfaction you feel with your life. It is easy to fill your life with things to do, even leisure activities. However, not all of these potential activities will give you a sense of satisfaction. This is because not all activities are important to you. If you are going to use your precious time, you should choose an activity that is of high value to you.

How do you know what activities would contribute the most to improving the quality of your life? We often do not think about what we value as we go through our busy day and the question of what a person values can often be confounding to them. Borrowing from a particular therapy called Acceptance and Commitment Therapy, we have included here an exercise in values clarification that will help you decide which activities would be of the greatest value to you.

The goal of this exercise is to identify ways you can put into your life the things that you value the most. The purpose of doing this is to improve your quality of life by having more things in your life that matter to you the most.

When we refer to the things you value, we are not referring to a specific activity. For example, you may have a value related to spending more time with your family. A specific activity that might flow from this value is to have a meal with your family once a week.

Below is a diagram that contains labels for various life domains. A life domain is an area of your life that reflects one portion of who you are and what you do. This is an example of what we are talking about when we refer to your life domain map.

Values clarification exercise for choosing preferred activities

Step 1 involves you listing as many life domains as you can think of that are relevant to you. We have included some life domains that people often list, but feel free to change them and add new ones that are relevant for you. What you are doing here is building your life domain map. Take your time to think up as many life domains as you understand to be part of your life. Other examples might be travel, exercise, etc.

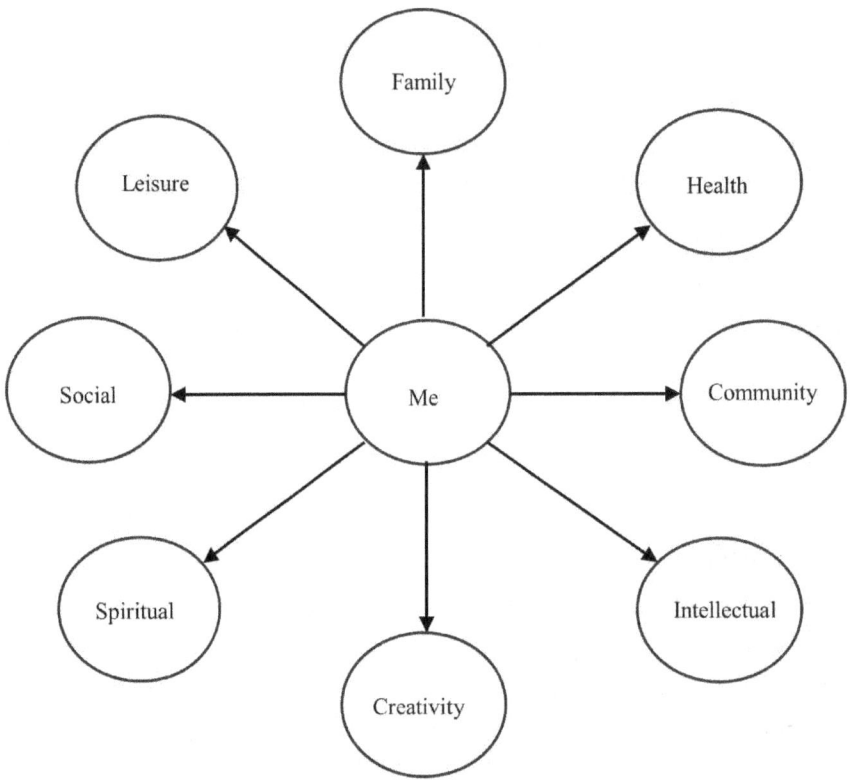

Figure 7: Example of a life domain map.

Step 2 involves you identifying what you already have in your life for the various life domains. Remember, list the values you have (e.g., ample time with my family) rather than specific activities (e.g., Sunday lunch with my family). You will begin to notice that some domains in your life have received lots of attention but other domains have received little or no attention. Here is an example of the types of values that might appear in the family domain.

> Family domain:
>
> > Time with family
> >
> > Special time with individual family members
> >
> > Spending time with the young members of my family
> >
> > Important family gatherings

Remember, you are listing here what you already have of value in your life with regard to this domain. This is not a list of the things you would like to have available to you.

Step 3 involves you now considering the things you would like to have in your life in each of the domains. Again, focus on the values (e.g., more quality time with my parents) rather than activities (e.g., visiting my parents on Sunday afternoons).

At this point, you will begin to notice several things.

> You will see that there are domains of your life that receive lots of attention already and you want very little else in that domain. Things in these domains are already satisfactory so there is limited purpose in focusing your attention on them.
>
> You will see that there are domains of your life where you have very little but you also do not really want very much more. These do not deserve your attention either.
>
> Importantly, you will see there are domains of your life where you have very little and there are many things that you want in that domain that you do not already have available to you. Focusing your attention of these would give you the greatest benefit.

It is the third type of life domain that will become the focus of attention from here on. This is because this focus will have the greatest chance of having the most important impact on the quality of your life.

<u>Step 4</u> involves you focusing on those life domains where you do not have enough of what matters to you and there is very much more that you want to include in your life. In this step, you should consider how those values that you want to put into your life might translate into specific activities. It is here that the 'what to do' component of the exercise occurs. For example, if you have a value associated with spending more time with your family, you might now consider ways that could happen by identifying specific activities you could engage in that would bring that value into your life (e.g., arranging family get-togethers, organising an online shared family photo site where family members can post photos for all family members to see).

<u>Step 5</u> involves identifying any barriers that might prevent you from engaging in these activities that would bring the things that you value into your life and finding ways around these barriers. For example, you may not be able to catch up in person with family members if they live in places distant from you, but you could overcome this barrier by arranging video chat get-togethers.

Of course, there will be things you want that are of value to you that you just cannot have because of real limitations. For example, you may like to travel but you cannot do so because you have too many demands placed on your time. However, if travel is of high value, then the quality of your life might be enhanced by spending time exploring places online or watching travel documentaries. Although not exactly what you would give the highest value, these activities are still related to the thing that matters to you.

Remember that your goal is to introduce into your life activities that are of high value to you that will improve the quality of your life. If you are going to devote the time to engaging in these types of activities, it will matter that you focus on the activities that are associated with your highest values.

Some final points

Below are some final points that need to be made or restated.

> You are one person and there are only so many hours in the day. You cannot keep giving yourself more to do and taking on more without reaching a limit.
>
> You cannot function in 'high gear' all the time without rest.
>
> Others will have an expectation that you will do more if you always say yes when asked to do something.
>
> No one can read your mind. You need to communicate what is happening to you if you want things to change.
>
> When you feel you have no more time, you can learn to manage your time differently so that demands on you are not so overwhelming.
>
> You should pay attention to what your nervous system is telling you. It will send you messages that you have pushed yourself too far.
>
> Life must be about more than hard work.

We wish you well for the future.

Additional reading

Eifer, G.H., Forsyth, J.P., & Hayes, S.C. (2005). *Acceptance and commitment therapy for anxiety disorders.* New York: New Harbinger Publications.

Kennerley, H., Kirk, J., & Westbrook, D. (2016). *An introduction to cognitive behaviour therapy: Skills and applications (3rd edn.).* London: Sage Publications.

Paterson, R.J. (2023). *The assertiveness workbook: How to express your ideas and stand up for yourself at work and in relationships.* London: New Harbinger Publications.

Tobin, D., Holroyd, K., Reynolds, R., & Wigal, J.K. (1989). The hierarchical structure of the Coping Strategies Inventory. *Cognitive Therapy and Research, 13(4),* 343-361.

www.ingramcontent.com/pod-product-compliance
Lightning Source LLC
Chambersburg PA
CBHW080856090426
42735CB00014B/3164